Jonathan McKee's parenting tips are powerful, thought-provoking, effective, and convicting—yet spiked with such humor and self-effacing sketches that his truths don't shame us for *our* ineffective parenting. They just make us want to do better.

— Rick Bundschuh, parent, pastor, author of *Deep Like Me*

Candid Confessions of an Imperfect Parent takes a fresh and authentic approach to parenting. I loved Jonathan's transparency. He motivated me to be a better parent—and I feel better knowing there are other imperfect parents like me.

— Jim Burns, president, HomeWord; author of *Confident Parenting* and *Faith Conversations for Families*

Jonathan is refreshingly transparent about his own lack of parenting skills. He weaves together his personal stories and those of many others into a tapestry that gives us a clear view of our messed-up world. But he doesn't leave us there. He offers hope, practical help, and encouragement. The good news for any parent is it is never too late to begin a solid relationship with your sons and daughters.

— Les Christie, author; chairman, Youth Ministry Department, William Jessup University

Candid Confessions of an Imperfect Parent is one of the most practical, most transparent, and most helpful parenting books I've ever read. As the parent of two teenagers myself, I feel better equipped after reading this book, and I think you will too. Buy a copy for yourself, and a few to give away, because you won't want to loan yours out!

— Kurt Johnston, pastor to students, Saddleback Church

Jonathan—imperfect parent that he is—shows you how to truly connect with your kid. He brings research and experience and delivers with amazing storytelling and humor.

— Dr. Kevin Leman, author of *Have a New Kid by Friday*

There is so much guilt that accompanies parenting, particularly if you are a Christian. Jonathan McKee takes the pressure off the pursuit of perfection and leads us to practical insight and hope for building into our kids the best we have to offer. You'll be a better parent after reading this book. I highly recommended it.

> — Mark Matlock, vice president, Youth Specialties; author of *Real World Parents* and *Raising Wise Children*

Every parent should read *Candid Confessions of an Imperfect Parent* to bridge the communication gap between parents and youth today. Jonathan's practical and easy-to-implement ideas are peppered with humor and common sense, which makes for an enjoyable and quick read. I recommend this book to all parents who would like to build relationships, or improve their relationships, with their teenagers.

> — Al Menconi, author, *But It Doesn't Affect Me*

Jonathan McKee is insightful, witty, authentic, and honest. This is a practical and lighthearted book that will help all parents value what's really important in life—a deepening relationship with our kids. I highly recommend this book.

> — Dr. David Olshine, director of Youth Ministry, Family, and Culture, Columbia International University

The cat's out of the bag: people who write parenting books aren't necessarily the perfect parents they let on to be! Not too many of us are willing to admit that, but Jonathan McKee transparently owns up to his own imperfections and suggests that imperfect parents are actually in the *perfect* position to become great parents. Jonathan makes his points quickly and illustrates them well with precision and good humor. I will recommend this book—especially to parents who don't like to read parenting books!

> — Wayne Rice, cofounder of Youth Specialties; author of *Generation to Generation* and *Engaging Parents as Allies*

CANDID CONFESSIONS OF AN IMPERFECT PARENT

BUILDING RELATIONSHIPS, BUYING BREAKFASTS, AND OTHER SECRETS FOR CONNECTING WITH YOUR TEENAGER

JONATHAN McKEE

Standard®
PUBLISHING
Bringing The Word to Life

Cincinnati, Ohio

Published by Standard Publishing, Cincinnati, Ohio
www.standardpub.com

Printed in the United States of America

Editors: Dale Reeves, Robert Irvin
Cover and interior design: Thinkpen Design, Inc., www.thinkpendesign.com

Published in association with the literary agency of Greg Johnson, WordServe Literary
Group, 10152 S. Knoll Circle, Highlands Ranch, CO 80130.

ISBN 978-0-7847-3184-0

Library of Congress Cataloging-in-Publication Data
McKee, Jonathan R. (Jonathan Ray), 1970-
  Candid confessions of an imperfect parent : building relationships, buying break-
fasts, and other secrets for connecting with your teenager / Jonathan McKee.
    p. cm.
  Includes bibliographical references.
  ISBN 978-0-7847-3184-0 (perfect bound)
  1. Parent and teenager--Religious aspects--Christianity. 2. Parenting--Religious
aspects--Christianity. 3. Child rearing--Religious aspects--Christianity. I. Title.
  BV4529.M3847 2011
  248.8'45--dc22
                          2010052318

16 15 14 13 12 11   9 8 7 6 5 4 3 2 1

CONTENTS

ACKNOWLEDGMENTS

THIS BOOK HAS BEEN A unique one, a work more vulnerable than anything I've previously written. It required transparency, and not just from me but from my whole family. I've given my kids drafts of the book multiple times asking for their opinion. "Is this OK? Does this represent you authentically?"

My kids have been incredible through this entire process, not only giving me their feedback but also allowing me to air our family's dirty laundry. I'm a little choked up even thinking about it.

So thank you Alec, my little buddy. I love you. I hope our relationship grows stronger each day. (And you're a far better writer than me. I look forward to your book.)

Thanks Alyssa, you funny girl. I love you and I look forward to more trips to the mall with you to look at shoes. (On the clearance rack!)

Thanks Ashley, you goofball! You and I are waaaaaaay too much alike. It's scary. I look forward to staying up late to watch scary movies with you. (And then telling you, "NO! You can't sleep with us! No more scary movies if you're going to do this! Now go back to your room!")

And Lori, my love of twenty years. You're amazing in every way! I couldn't have done this without you! Thanks for being my number one fan (in a total, non-Kathy Bates-kind of way).

I want to give a special shout-out to several of my friends who read this book in its early stages, commented, and helped me massage it into form. Thanks Julie, Todd, David, Lane, and Danette!

And thanks to Jim Burns and Greg Johnson for making this book happen! I appreciate your help more than you'll ever know!

God, it's only by your love and grace that any of this is possible. Thanks for loving me, despite my imperfections!

I'LL NEVER DO THAT WITH *MY* KIDS . . .

ON A QUIET EVENING, YEARS before becoming a parent, my wife Lori and I went grocery shopping together. As we pushed the shopping cart down the cereal aisle, we couldn't help but notice the mom screaming at her four-year-old: "Stop grabbing things off the shelf!"

The mom resumed her shopping, only to discover, seconds later, her child grabbing the cereal box again.

Mom barked again. "I said stop grabbing that box or you've got another thing coming!"

Lori snuck a glance at me, wide-eyed. We both feigned shopping while eagerly watching the in-store entertainment.

The child patiently waited for mom to turn around before grabbing the cereal box again. This time the kid started biting on the box, picking at the sealed opening with his fingers, even banging it on the cart like a sea otter desperately trying to open a clam.

Lori's mouth fell open in dismay. Meanwhile, I searched for some popcorn. This was better than any movie.

After what seemed like minutes, the clueless mom finally noticed the child playing with the box of cereal. She sighed and looked up at us who, by this time, were both staring openmouthed at this circus act. She shrugged her shoulders, simply said "Kids!", and resumed shopping with her child—who was victoriously holding onto his sugar-saturated prize.

"I can't believe some parents!" I said to my wife as we rounded the corner. "No wonder so many kids have discipline problems today. I'll never do that with my kids!"

Then I had Alec.

Alec and I would enjoy the days in engaging conversation.

"Alec, no! Alec! Daddy said no! Alec, Daddy said NO! Now don't make me come over there!"

Alec would eventually comply.

There! Not bad. I knew I could handle this parenting thing.

Then I had Alyssa.

The conversations grew even more intellectually stimulating.

"Alyssa, no! Alyss . . . Alec, Daddy will handle Alyssa. You just worry about yourself, OK? Thank you. You're such a good big brother.

"Alyssa, no! Alyssa, NO! Alyss . . . oh . . . oh no . . . Alyssa sweetie, don't cry. Alyssa, it's OK. Please don't cry. Alyssa-lyssa-lyssa-lyssa sweetie! Alyssa-ditta-ditta-ditta-baby-doll!"

Alyssa and Alec both eventually composed themselves.

"There. Good girl. See, it's not so bad. You just need to listen when Daddy says no, OK? Good girl."

Whew! Not bad. I think I can handle this parenting thing.

Then I had Ashley.

I think it would be fair to say that communication had digressed at a measurable rate. A typical conversation with all three of them:

"Ashley, no! Leave Alyssa alone.

"ALYSSA! Don't hit your sister! Alyss . . . oh . . . oh no . . . Alyssa sweetie, don't cry. Oh . . . hold on Lyssa-sweetie.

"Alec—NO! Get off the counter! I don't care if you're thirsty—get off the counter! I don . . . hold on . . .

"Ashley, get away from the cat! ASHLEY! I SAID GET AWAY FROM THE . . . CAT! Oh Ashley . . . oh no . . . Ashley sweetie, don't cry.

"Alyssa . . . no, not you too. Alyssa sweetie, don't cry. . . . ALEC, I THOUGHT I SAID GET OFF THE COUNTER!

"Oh . . . no, I wasn't yelling at you girls. Don't cry.

"Alec . . . oh no. Alec, please don't cry.

"Would just *one* of you please stop crying?!!"

Sigh.

And they aren't even teenagers yet. Anybody got any clue how to do this parenting thing?

A PARADIGM SHIFT

What looked easy from the sidelines has proven to be more difficult than I could have ever imagined. Everything changed when we had kids of our own—it's a paradigm shift all parents experience. Now *I am* that screaming mother in the grocery store. There are times that I've thought of just giving up and giving my kid "the cereal box." (It's the easy way out—in the heat of the moment.) And when they grow into teenagers, it doesn't get any easier. A cereal box is just replaced by an Xbox, Facebook, or an iPhone—or all of the above.

Experiences like these always leave me wondering if anyone has any real answers. Does anyone actually have this parenting thing nailed?

I always find it entertaining when some young adult—someone with no kids—attempts to give parents actual parenting advice. That's like a guy who has never left Nebraska trying to teach mountain climbing. There are some things you just have to experience. My twenty years of youth ministry experience and my hundreds of hours of youth culture research pale in comparison to the frontline challenges I've experienced as the parent of three teenagers. Those of you who are the parents of teens know exactly what I'm talking about. I have three teenagers of my own, a sink full of dishes, really high car insurance, and a head full of gray hairs. *Ya feel me?*

If I told you I was a perfect parent, four people in my house would burst out laughing. If I told you I had all the answers, I probably couldn't even keep a straight face. It's been a long haul. But by God's grace, despite my imperfections, my wife Lori and I have three amazing kids. Perfect kids? Not even close. But last night we actually all sat around the living room, hanging out, laughing, talking, and finally praying together before we went to bed. We truly enjoy each other's company. In our family, if I mention the words "family night," my kids actually don't moan and complain. (It's kinda weird!)

I can't thank God enough for my family.

This book is a glimpse inside the world of an imperfect family—but a *family*. We have plenty of issues, and my kids are facing pressures and temptations that I never dreamed of. Lori and I have spent countless nights questioning our decisions, reflecting, second-guessing some more, wondering, and sometimes just crying. It's hard to even try verbalizing the vested love that parents pour into their children.

Imperfect parents.

Imperfect kids.

An imperfect world.

Still, Lori and I keep trying daily. We are always looking for opportunities to build stronger relationships with our kids and open the door to teach lasting values. Hopefully, with this book, you can gain a few insights from our successes and failures along this tumultuous journey. Or, at the very least . . . you can enjoy the ride—at my expense!

THE QUESTIONS IN THIS BOOK

At the end of each chapter, I've provided questions to ponder. So you can get candid with yourself, your spouse, a group, or all of the above! That's why—cleverly, I thought—I called them Candid Questions for Reflection. I think they'll work equally well if you go through them on your own, with your spouse, or in a parent or reading club group.

JONATHAN MCKEE, IMPERFECT PARENT

BLEMISHED

(LIFE LESSONS)

I DON'T KNOW EXACTLY HOW the fight started, but I remember how it ended. While my wife Lori and I were screaming at each other behind a closed bedroom door, a piece of paper began feeding from under the door, as if we were receiving a fax from the hallway.

Lori and I silenced mid-scream.

Isn't it amazing how you can do that? Yelling one moment, then the phone rings and you answer it with a textbook friendly "Hello?" like the world is a perfect place.

I wandered over to the door and retrieved the "fax."

It was inscribed in crayon:

PLEEZ STOP FITING.

I guess the kids *did* hear. I had been repressing that reality. That made we wonder who else had heard. I began picturing one of these notes feeding from under the front door from our next-door neighbor.

I stared at the note for a few seconds.

For a brief moment I remember thinking, *Wow, my six-year-old's spelling is atrocious!*

Lori and I didn't have many fights like that, but we had enough to make me wonder if the kids still remember those days when the doors closed and the voices grew louder and louder. It's embarrassing to admit.

I guess I could try to blame it on my Irish temper, and my wife could blame it on . . . well . . . my Irish temper, but that would be a cop-out. The fact is that I let my temper get the best of me too many times. It hurt Lori, it hurt me, and I'd be stupid to deny its effect on my kids.

I'm as imperfect as they come.

So is that it? Am I doomed to fail at parenting? Should I just give up now?

BLEMISHED—BUT NOT ALONE

Ever buy at the clearance rack?

You can add "cheapskate" to my many attributes. Whenever I walk into a store, I immediately look for the clearance rack. I guess I'm not too cheap, because I do like quality brands. I just don't pay for these brands unless I get them at 50 to 70 percent off. This usually means that I'm buying last season's clothes, or something "blemished" or "imperfect."

One of my favorite outlet stores always has a "blemished rack." These are the same name-brand shirts and pants that are being sold at full price, but the ones on this rack are marked *blemished* because of some imperfection. It's interesting to look through the rack because sometimes it's nearly impossible to find the imperfection in the product.

I once saw a pair of pants that were exactly what I was looking for and just my size (with the waist a few inches bigger than when I was first married). I pulled the pants off the hanger and began searching for the blemish. I checked the stitching in the front and back. The buttons seemed normal and the belt loops appeared equally spaced and intact. (Can you tell that I look at this rack a lot?) The seams looked good running down the leg, and the length of each leg was the same.

I figured the imperfection had to be something with the fit. So I took them into the dressing room and tried them on. They fit great. They actually made me look skinnier than I wasn't.

I walked out of the dressing room and posed for Lori like Jim Carrey in his tux in *Dumb and Dumber*. "Whadaya think?"

"You're a nerd," she quickly retorted. "But I like the jeans!"

I took them off and investigated them again. I really wanted these jeans, and they were an excellent price.

Where was the blemish?

I finally gave up my search and brought them to the cashier. "Where's the blemish?"

The cashier looked up from behind the counter where she was folding clothes, took one glimpse at the jeans, and said, "Oh, stick your hands in the pockets."

"Huh?"

She spoke a little slower this time. "Stick . . . your . . . hands . . . in . . . the . . . pockets."

I shoved my hand in the right front pocket and it stopped mid-knuckle. The cashier smiled, didn't say a word, and went back to folding clothes.

I CHUCKLED TO MYSELF. *THE PANTS DON'T HAVE DEEP POCKETS. PERFECT. NEITHER DO I. THAT'S WHY I'M SHOPPING AT THE STINKING BLEMISHED RACK!*

We are blemished—every single one of us. That doesn't mean that we're not of good quality, or not worthy of being a parent; it just means that we need some guidance. The question is, are we willing to accept guidance? (The fact that you're reading a book on parenting is a great sign that you're open to advice.)

Everyone makes mistakes. Growth as a parent begins when we learn from our mistakes. Learning from these life experiences results in wisdom. Let me put it another way. Our blemishes create opportunities to become all the wiser.

In the Bible, the apostle Paul spent the first three chapters of the book of Romans trying to get his readers to accept the fact all people are flawed. He quoted Old Testament passages to remind them that this idea is nothing new. "There is no one righteous, not even one" (Romans 3:10, citing Psalm 14:3).

But that's a good thing.

OK . . . maybe that came out wrong. What I mean to say is, our blemishes aren't good, but it's a good thing that we aren't alone in this predicament. If you're feeling imperfect, understand that you aren't the only one. There is no such thing as the perfect parent.

I find it refreshing to know that we're not alone in this. If we continue reading in Romans, we'll see that not only are we all blemished, but also that God loves us in spite of our imperfections. Don't stop at chapter 3 of Romans. Keep reading and you'll see how God loves us, *blemishes and all*. In Romans 5 Paul reminds us that God knew how messed up we were when he sent his Son Jesus to die for us (v. 8).

But it all starts with understanding that we are blemished.

OWNING UP

That's one of the big problems with the world today. Many people want to justify everything, or deny it, or cover it up . . . instead of just owning up and admitting, "I made a mistake." And learning from that mistake.

Over the last year and a half golfer Tiger Woods has learned that lesson the hard way. *Fast Company* magazine's Joel Rubinson said it well in an article a couple of weeks after Woods's famous car-crash incident on Thanksgiving 2009:

> Tiger makes $100 million or more per year from endorsements—more the result of his personal brand than his golf swing. His brand transcends the sport. He is The Natural, and he gives youth to a sport that skews old in its demos. His squeaky clean image made him a no-brainer for marketers and ad agencies. None of this really changed when he smashed his car driving

down a residential street he'd driven hundreds of times before or even because there was something fishy about the whole incident; it changed because he stonewalled.

In an era of social media, the table-stakes of branding are honesty, openness, and transparency. We all knew something happened, and we knew *brand Woods* should talk about it, explain it, let us forgive him for it. And we probably *would* have forgiven him, but now we can't even consider that without smirking and thinking of him as fodder for Letterman's top 10 and tabloid headlines about "the back nine."[1]

Many theorize that Tiger wouldn't have lost multiple sponsors if only he had owned up to his infidelity. The cover-up is what cost him, and it cost him big time.

We need to admit our mistakes and learn from them. This is a problem that not only affects multi-millionaire athletes.

My friends recently adopted a little boy. This four-year-old is a delight. He loves wrestling with his new dad, playing with his new sisters, and he's as smart as a whip. Top it off with a warm, engaging personality—a lot of fun packed into that little four-year-old frame.

Because I knew his history I was actually surprised when I met him the first time and saw firsthand how pleasant he is. This little kid had had it rough.

His mom was an avid drug user. When she first had her son, she quickly learned of a county program where you could drop off your kid for several weeks for personal reasons, no questions asked. She maxed out her time every instance, picking up her son one day before the maximum time allowed. After the minimum number of days passed, she would drop him off again. This happened like clockwork.

Soon the county grew wise to her quality of parenting (don't make me tell you how long this took) and they put the child in foster care. This slap in the face seemed to shake up the mom. She visited the caseworker in charge and pleaded her case, promising she would change.

Here's where I wish the story had a happy ending for her.

Unfortunately, she didn't learn from her mistakes.

She was given opportunities to take custody of her son for a few days at a time. The county scheduled some dates during these custodial periods for a caseworker to come and check out her living situation and assess what kind of home she could provide for her son.

Time to clean house, right?

When the county workers showed up, the house was a wreck, including a crack pipe on the coffee table within the toddler's reach.

Not good.

You'd think she'd have learned her lesson by that point, right?

Well, you know the ending to this story. My friend now has this little boy. This boy's mother was given so much grace, time and time again, and she failed to learn from her mistakes. Because of this, she lost her child.

She had opportunities to "clean house" several times.

She never did.

Very sad for her.

Very good for this little boy.

We need to learn from our mistakes.

Most of us haven't made as many parenting mistakes as this little boy's mom did. But even if you have, grace is still available.

CONFESSION TIME

I've made a ton of mistakes in my years as a parent. My two daughters and my son would probably attest to that!

One of the biggest mistakes I've made as a parent was being too impatient with my son Alec (he'd agree with this wholeheartedly). Alec and I have very different personalities. Even though we're both slightly nerdy, like movies, and joke very similarly, we are complete opposites in "drive." I'm an entrepreneur and a go-getter. Alec is . . . I'll quote him . . . "chill."

When I was about twelve, I pushed a lawn mower all around my neighborhood, knocking on doors and offering to mow a neighbor's lawn one week for free to show them what a good job I'd do. Before long, I had a handful of weekly lawn jobs.

Whenever those fund-raising guys would come to our elementary school and motivate us with contests to see who could raise the most money in pledges or sell the most magazines, I wanted to be number one. I usually was in the running.

In junior high our school had a canned food drive. Some kids brought in ten cans. Some brought in a couple. Others brought none. I brought in almost two hundred. I went around the neighborhood with a wheelbarrow collecting cans because I wanted to collect the most.

This is who I am.

My son is not me.

It took me a while to realize that this is OK.

I'd say things like: "What do you mean you don't want to go get some lawn jobs? When I was a kid, I pushed the mower around the neighborhood . . ."

I think you get the picture.

On any given day I'd get home and Alec would be sitting, playing video games for hours upon hours if I didn't limit his game time. I tried to be creative at first. "Hey Alec. I'll give you ten dollars to go wash the car."

Alec would pause his game and think for a minute. *Ten dollars? Hmmmmm.* Then he'd clarify. "Are you telling me that I *have* to do it?"

"No," I'd quickly explain. "But if you do, you'll get ten dollars." And then I sweetened the deal. "Plus tip!"

He'd lay his head back on the couch lethargically and look up at the ceiling. "So, I can wash the car and get ten dollars . . ." He paused, slowly processing it out loud. "Or, keep playing video games."

"Yes. Ten dollars. Plus tip," I said, knowing what I would have chosen, in a heartbeat, if I were his age.

"No thanks," he'd finally conclude. "I'll just keep playing video games. But thanks, Dad."

I blew up!

Ten minutes later, when I finished my loud, long-winded, condescending lecture about laziness, Alec would end up outside washing the car anyway . . . *for free!*

This kind of stuff went on frequently. Lori would graciously tell me, "Jonathan, you mean well, and your principles aren't wrong, but you need to cut the kid a break. Alec isn't like you."

"I know, but . . ." I'd argue, knowing all too well that she was right, but trying to retain some dignity.

"He's a good boy, Jonathan," Lori fired back. "He's sweet, he gets good grades, he doesn't do drugs, he loves God, he's polite, adults love him . . . and yes . . . he's also pretty chill. Let it go."

I confessed to my guy's accountability group that I was being too hard on my son. My good friend who had spent many evenings with our family laughed with me as I explained the situation. He's witnessed some of these moments personally. He said honestly, "Yeah, I've felt pretty sorry for Alec during some of those long lectures."

It was a fact. My impatience kept snaring me again and again.

I needed to clean house.

Owning up to the mistake is a good thing. Confessing it to others and seeking help is even better. But there's one key principle that is still missing.

We can't do this by our own power.

UNLESS THE LORD BUILDS THE HOUSE

In Psalm 127:1, Solomon shared some enlightening words of wisdom. He said:

UNLESS THE LORD BUILDS THE HOUSE, ITS BUILDERS LABOR IN VAIN.

For years I tried to use "human" tools to correct my problem with my son. *Count to ten. Pick your battles. Keep accountable to my friends.* All very good things.

But ultimately, all of them worthless . . . *unless God is in it.*

When we do it on our own, we're simply declaring to God, "Thanks for your offer to help, but I got this!" In other words, "Leave me alone, God; I'm doing this one on my own."

That's pride.

PRIDE KILLS. THAT'S NOT MEANT AS JUST A PITHY SAYING; IT'S TRUE. HEALTHY HOMES ARE STIFLED AND CHOKED BY THE KIND OF PRIDE THAT CONVINCES A PARENT THAT "EVERYTHING'S FINE."

If you meet a parent who claims "everything's fine," something stinky is usually locked in the cellar. Healthy healing in a home begins when a parent is big enough to admit to God, "I give up! I need your help."

Unless the Lord builds your house, you labor in vain. God wants to help you and me with our parenting. Let's not be so vain to say, "I got this!" We're imperfect. We're blemished. We don't "got this!" We need him in the process every step of the way.

You might be thinking, *Hey, I thought this was a parenting book, not a sermon.*

Simply put, this is a confession from an imperfect parent. I'm as shrewd as they come (apparently pretty cocky too), but I couldn't do this on my own. I tried. There were some pretty tense moments in my house—and still are at times. These struggles always require me to bring this to God and confess, "I don't have this. Matter of fact, I need you to take this!"

It starts with owning that we're imperfect. Then confess it to God and others. Then give God the reins.

That might sound cliché, so let me quickly put some feet to that.

For me, giving God the reins was much more than just singing "Jesus Take the Wheel." I found two common practices very helpful. These might seem overly simple. But as Da Vinci pointed out, "Simplicity is the ultimate sophistication."[2]

Give it to God in prayer

Yeah, I know. Duh!

I'm not talking about saying grace before dinner or praying for the missionaries on your fridge. I mean getting alone with God the way Jesus instructed in Matthew 6:6 when he taught us how to pray. He actually told us to go find a place by ourselves and talk to God: "But when you pray, go into your room, close the door and pray to your Father, who is unseen." Then, a few verses later, he instructed us to pray, "Your will be done" (v. 10).

GOD WANTS TO HELP US. WHAT BETTER WAY TO SURRENDER TO HIM THAN TO GO AWAY BY OURSELVES AND TELL HIM, "GOD, I'M GIVING THIS PARENTING THING TO YOU. IT'S TOO BIG FOR ME. IT'S ALL YOURS. CHANGE ME TO BE MORE LIKE YOU."

Some of us might even want to lift up special requests at this time. "God, if you could just help me with my temper. If you would just set off an alarm in my head when I'm about to blow. Help me to flee that temptation."

Do you think God will honor that request? Why not give it a try and see?

Fill your head with the wisdom of Scripture

Yeah, I know. Duh!

The Bible is full of advice that translates to our parenting. I recently went through the book of 1 Peter with my wife and some friends. I was amazed how every week I learned principles that could carry over to my relationship with Alec and his sisters Alyssa and Ashley. First Peter is filled with encouragement to fill ourselves with Christ and live lives of self-control so that others will see Christ in us.

Isn't that what we want as parents?

It all starts with filling our heads with the truth.

Lori and I began "filling our heads with the truth" of God's Word together as a family after dinner—as often as possible. Some people call this time devotions. This word, "devotions," is just a fancy rendering for reading the Bible—which is God's Word to us. Our family probably does this about four or five nights a week. We started in Genesis, then skipped to 1 Peter. We hit the Gospels, then Philippians. As I write this, we're going through Ephesians.

Lori and I can see the impact of the truth of the Word in all of our lives. Don't neglect the opportunity to fill yourselves with it.

There are many more ideas in the box below. So, if you're imperfect like me and you're looking for answers, you might want to give some of these simple practices a try.

IDEAS FOR FILLING OUR HEADS WITH THE TRUTH

- Read through the book of Genesis, one chapter at a time. This book gives a solid foundation for God's love for us and how we as humans repeatedly stray from what he wants.
- Read through the book of Proverbs in a month, one chapter per day. This book is full of great wisdom—practical applications for day-to-day living.
- Change it up and read a topical book that deals with biblical truths relevant for the whole family.
- For teens, read a hard-hitting yet relevant book together, something like Francis Chan's *Crazy Love* or a book by John Ortberg (a good one is *If You Want to Walk on Water, You've Got to Get Out of the Boat*). These books offer ready-made quick lessons that you can read together with both Scripture and application.
- Read the Gospel of Mark, one chapter at a time. This book provides an amazing look at Jesus and his love for the people he encountered.
- Read the book of Acts, one chapter at a time. In this book, we get to see how the followers of Jesus began spreading the truth and meeting together to encourage each other.
- Read a book on evangelism like Greg Stier's amazing *You're Next!* Books like these will not only challenge your family to share God's love with others, they also equip *you* to do it.
- Read through 1 Peter just half a chapter at a time. This short New Testament book has great insight on what it means to live holy lives during tough times.
- Read through 1 John half a chapter at a time. This tiny New Testament book provides amazing application for living out our love for God by loving others.

Maybe, like me, you've also tried some human tools to build your spiritual house, and it was in vain. What good are tools when they aren't in the hands of the master carpenter, Jesus? "Unless the Lord builds the house" . . . we labor in vain.

ANYONE ELSE IMPERFECT?

Perhaps you've never received a crayon fax from your kids begging you to stop fighting. If your kids brought home a bad report card, maybe you didn't overreact; instead you just stopped, prayed, then gave your daughter a noogie and took her to ice cream. Maybe you're Mary Poppins, the perfect disciplinarian. If so . . . you can skip this book. Because I'm as imperfect as they get. But by God's grace, I've somehow managed to build close relationships with my two daughters and my son, trying to teach them lasting values along the way.

If you're imperfect, you're in good company. Many of the truths I've learned are from the school of hard knocks. In other words: "Oooops. That sure didn't work. Let me take note of that for the future." My history as a father is smattered with blowups and bad decisions. The key was learning from each of those instances.

I'd be lying if I told you that being a parent has been an easy road. It's put more gray hairs on my head than a bottle of hair color ever could cover. And God's not through working with me yet. But with prayer, accountability, and a lot of grace, it's become a little more "chill" in the McKee house in recent years.

If you've made mistakes in the past, don't give up. God wants to use you to make a difference in the lives of your kids—whether they're very young or teenagers.

Right about now, you might be wondering, *How much of a difference can a parent really make?*

That's what chapter 2 is about.

• CANDID QUESTIONS FOR REFLECTION •

Some Questions for You, You & Your Spouse, or Your Small Group to Ponder

1. **WHAT BLEMISHES** or imperfections do you struggle with as a parent?

2. **RECALL A** time when you tried to cover up your imperfections. How did that work for you? Share the story with your spouse or with others if in a group.

3. **IS THERE** a time when you learned from a parenting mistake, improving the next time around? What happened?

4. **AS A** parent, in what area—or areas—might you need to "clean house" right now?

5. **WHAT ARE** some reasons why people try to fix their imperfections on their own instead of giving them to God?

6. **IN WHAT** *specific* ways could you improve your communication with God through prayer?

7. **WHAT ARE** some ways you could make reading the Bible a priority for your family? Which one will you try this week?

8. **HOW CAN** you relinquish one of your parenting struggles to God this week? What does that actually look like, tomorrow and the next day?

BUILDING
RELATIONSHIPS

2

CAN I EVEN MAKE A DIFFERENCE?

(THE WEIGHT OF PARENTAL INFLUENCE)

IN JANUARY 2010, THE KAISER Family Foundation (KFF) released a study that will continue to be quoted and cited by newspapers and other medical studies for years to come. The report was titled "Generation M2: Media in the Lives of 8- to 18-Year-Olds," and it unveiled exactly how much "entertainment media" kids are absorbing daily.

The average? Seven hours, 38 minutes a day.

Sound like a lot? Hold on. That's far from all.

The study dug a little deeper and noted a trend called "media multitasking." An example of this is when a kid is browsing the Web while listening to music at the same time. KFF inquired about that tendency and found that kids actually cram a total of 10 hours and 45 minutes of different media into the span of 7 hours and 38 minutes.

That's a lot of MTV, iTunes, and Facebook!

There's more.

That doesn't even include texting. No, texting is not considered "entertainment media" in this study. The foundation discovered that the average kid spends 1 hour and 35 minutes using his or her cell phone (for talking and texting), and thus, this hour and a half has to be added to the original 7 hours and 38 minutes. (For the study, the foundation is lumping all kids and teens, ages eight to eighteen, together.)

Bottom line: each day the average young person is staring at a TV, a computer monitor, a phone, or a magazine for a total of 12 hours and 20 minutes, crammed into 9 hours and 13 minutes.[3]

That's a full-time job . . . plus overtime!

When most of us who are parents see how much time kids are spending absorbing these messages from the media and friends, we wonder, *Can I even make a difference at all?*

It's a good question. Parents commonly wonder, *How can I compete?* We aren't as cool as Justin Timberlake or as fashionable as Katy Perry. Besides, the messages from the media are basically summed up by "Live for the moment, do what's fun, and who cares?!" Parents' messages come back to "Think about your future, do what's wise, and your choices have consequences, both good and bad."

Which voice did you listen to when you were sixteen?

And think, you didn't hear half the media messages that they do today. When KFF did this report in 1999, that 12 hours and 20 minutes total was just 7 hours and 29 minutes. (I laugh at the word "just" there.) That's an increase of about 65 percent over those ensuing eleven years. (And I wonder what that number was in the 1980s, when I was a teenager!)

As parents we're often tempted to just throw up our hands and give up. What positive influence can we possibly make in a world where most kids are spending far more time with MTV and iTunes than with their parents? Can we really make an impact?

Do you really want to know?

Because the answer isn't just some feel-good phrase that someone made up. The answer is backed by research—across the board.

THE TRUTH IS: *YES, PARENTS MAKE AN OVERWHELMING DIFFERENCE.* AND ALMOST EVERY STUDY OUT THERE WILL PLEAD WITH PARENTS TO SPEND MORE TIME WITH THEIR CHILD, OPEN UP THE COMMUNICATION CHANNELS, AND HELP THEM LEARN TO MAKE GOOD DECISIONS.

I can't say it any more clearly. You can make a huge difference!

THE GREATEST INFLUENCE

Dr. Ross Campbell, MD, professor of pediatrics and psychiatry at University of Tennessee College of Medicine, wrote an amazing book titled *How to Really Love Your Child.* I can't emphasize it better than he did:

> Many parents feel no matter how good a job they do, their efforts have little overall effect upon their child. Just the opposite is true. Every study I've read indicates that the home wins hands down in every case. The influence of parents far outweighs everything else. The home holds the upper hand in determining how happy, secure, and stable a child is; how a child gets along with adults, peers, and different children; how confident a youngster is in himself and his abilities; how affectionate he is or how aloof; how he responds to unfamiliar situations. Yes, the home, despite many distractions for a child, has the greatest influence on him.[4]

As Dr. Campbell said, the home wins, hands down.

Is he alone in his assessment?

In September of 2010, The National Center on Addiction and Substance Abuse (CASA) published a study about the importance of family dinners. Why would a group of scholars doing research on drugs and alcohol abuse write a report about families getting together around the dinner table? I'll let them explain:

> Over the past 16 years, The National Center on Addiction and Substance Abuse at Columbia University has surveyed thousands of American teens and their parents to identify factors that increase or decrease the likelihood of teen substance abuse. We have learned that a child who gets

through age 21 without smoking, using illegal drugs or abusing alcohol is virtually certain never to do so. And, we've learned that parents have the greatest influence on whether their teens will choose to use.[5]

There it is again. "Parents have the greatest influence."

This study from CASA goes on to reveal that family dinners are one of the key ingredients in the lives of kids who stay drug-, alcohol-, and tobacco-free. In fact, the "more often children have dinners with their parents, the less likely they are to smoke, drink or use drugs."

The report details that those kids from families who have infrequent family dinners (fewer than three per week) are:

- Twice as likely to use tobacco
- Nearly twice as likely to use alcohol
- One and a half times likelier to use marijuana

CASA describes the family dinner as one of the most potent tools helping parents raise healthy, drug-free children. They conclude, "Simply put: frequent family dinners make a difference."[6]

ABSENT PARENTS

I've been a youth worker for longer than I've been a parent. (I've got one kid in college right now. Do the math: that's a long time.) And one thing that any youth worker will attest to is the value of a family support system in a teenager's life.

I remember a brother and sister who wandered into a campus outreach ministry I directed years ago.

TINA, ONLY THIRTEEN, WAS DRESSED LIKE AN EIGHTEEN-YEAR-OLD LOOKING FOR ATTENTION, AND TOM, FIFTEEN, WAS DRESSED LIKE A GANGSTA! AN INVESTMENT OF TIME EASILY BROKE THROUGH THAT TOUGH OUTER SHELL, AND I SOON DISCOVERED TWO AMAZING KIDS INSIDE.

Lori and I had these two in our home quite a bit. Their parents had split and they both lived mostly with their mom. Dad was in the picture sometimes—when he didn't forget that it was his weekend with the kids.

One Friday I called Tom to see if he wanted to come over for dinner (he usually spent Fridays alone because mom was barhopping). Tina answered the phone and informed me, "He's waiting outside for my dad."

"Oh." I thought about it for a moment. "You aren't waiting also?"

"Nope," she quickly answered. "He isn't going to show. I'm not wasting my time."

This had happened before.

I moved my phone to the other ear and looked at my watch. It was 4:45. "What time was he supposed to be there?"

"3:30." She was very matter-of-fact about it, munching on some chips as she talked.

"So . . ." I paused, not really knowing what to say. "Tom's still waiting?"

She finished chewing. "Yep. Pretty sad, huh?"

About 5:15 I pulled up to the house. Tom was sitting on the green electrical box in their front yard, throwing rocks at a light pole.

I rolled down my window. "Hey, Tom."

He looked up at me, looked at the time on his phone, then looked up at me again. "Hey," he finally managed.

"I've got a mad desire for pizza, and I hate eating alone," I offered.

It took Tom all of two seconds to make that decision. Ten minutes later we were laughing and playing video games in a pizza place by his house, waiting for our pizza to come out of the oven.

Tom's dad was the stereotypical "absent dad." And it eventually revealed itself in Tom's grades, his relationships, and his decisions.

Tom slipped in and out of my radar for the next few years. When he was sixteen he joined a third of the other kids in his neighborhood and dropped out of high school. When he was seventeen he got a girl pregnant and moved in with her. When he was eighteen I heard he was working at a local gas station. I don't know where he is today.

Tina didn't fare much better. Her clothes grew skimpier as she got older. She slept around frequently, thinking that was the trick to keeping guys. Eventually she dropped out of school too.

Tina and Tom grew up ignored. Their mom was too busy trying to find a man, and their dad was a flake. It was hard to watch. It was even more difficult as their lives began falling apart.

There were times when I would get late calls from Tom, asking me for advice or to come pick him up. I was all he had. His parents weren't there and he was searching for something stable in his life. I'd like to think that I helped him for a couple years, but I had two hundred kids at the time in the ministry I was serving in. About a hundred of them didn't have fathers in their lives.

The Toms and Tinas of this world would have a much better shot at life if they had a stable foundation at home—parents who invested in them.

TOM WAS NEVER TAUGHT HOW TO BE A MAN, SO HE FIGURED IT OUT BY HIMSELF. TINA WAS NEVER TAUGHT TO BE A LADY, SO SHE TOOK LESSONS FROM THE MEDIA.

For Tom and Tina, it's quite obvious, a dad and a mom who chose to be present would have made a huge difference.

Sadly, Tom and Tina's parents resolved that the kids could figure it out on their own. They did. And now Tom and Tina are statistics.

In my two decades of youth ministry I've seen hundreds of Toms and Tinas. Absent parents almost guarantee difficulty for the kids.

I've also seen a handful of exceptions. A teenager named Jason came from one of the worst homes I've ever seen, and somehow, he resolved to rise above it. He's an amazing young man today, married with a child of his own. I've seen the opposite as well. Good parents who did a fantastic job, only for their teenager to rebel and follow a path that led to plenty of pain and sorrow. But I'd be lying if I didn't tell you those were the exceptions. Loving, caring, present parents make a huge difference in almost every case.

IF YOU'RE A SINGLE MOM: PLENTY OF REASON TO HOPE

If you're a single mom and Dad isn't in your daughter's life, don't lose hope. You still can make a world of difference, providing love, nurturing, and a safe place where she feels noticed, heard, and appreciated. And don't underestimate the influence of other positive male role models in your daughter's life. I've seen numerous girls who bonded with their grandpa, stepdad, or uncle. Obviously, you want to be cautious, using great wisdom and discretion as you screen role models for your kids. Today's world has some pretty sick people in it. I'm sure I don't need to tell you—don't send your daughter off with the first man who pays her attention.

A decade ago I heard a pastor say these words: "Show me a girl who is dressed risqué and vying for guys to notice her, and I'll show you a girl who was ignored by her father." I reacted to his statement when I first heard it.

"How can you say that?" I argued. "Maybe she just watches too much MTV."

He simply replied, "Just take note. You'll see."

I walked away unconvinced. I didn't buy it.

Then I started to take note of the young girls in my ministry who dressed with overtly sexual overtones. (One thing made his theory a little difficult to measure, and that is—almost *all* girls dress overtly sexual these days. I know. I have two daughters and it's hard to find them clothes that actually cover them up!) But even in this risqué world with all its skimpy apparel, most would agree that some girls tend to dress more provocatively than others, and often make sexual comments, sometimes even advances. Every time I came across one of those girls, I tried to investigate the family situation. I was curious: Was Dad at home? Was he in their lives?

AS THE YEARS PASSED, THAT PASTOR'S WORDS RANG TRUE AGAIN AND AGAIN. NINE TIMES OUT OF TEN, IF A GIRL WAS VYING FOR SEXUAL ATTENTION, SHE HADN'T RECEIVED LOVE AND ATTENTION FROM HER FATHER. SHE DIDN'T KNOW WHAT DADDY'S HUG FELT LIKE.

She wasn't told that she was beautiful day after day by a man who was her biggest fan. So she slowly began to seek inappropriate male attention elsewhere.

Attention from Dad makes a huge difference. Sadly, the absent dad is becoming all too common.

I've seen this "Daddy void" again and again—sometimes when Dad is right in the next room. Just because a dad lives at a house doesn't necessarily guarantee his presence in his kids' lives. I've known many absent fathers who lived at home but were vacant emotionally and socially from their families. They're gone before the kids are up, home late each night, too tired to interact when they get home from work, and golfing or working all day on Saturdays.

Some of these dads actually drive to church on Sundays with big smiles on their faces, do church, drive home, watch football . . . and start all over again Monday morning.

Maybe you're thinking, *Jonathan, aren't you being a little harsh? Most parents aren't like this.*

Famed pediatrician Berry Brazelton, in the Robert Evans book *Family Matters*, noted: "A typical father will spend less than three minutes per day alone with a child who has reached his or her teenage years."[7] That's so unbelievably sad!

When I first read that statistic, I didn't have trouble believing it. In all honesty, I immediately thought, *Oh no! I hope I spend more than that!* And I started calculating it in my head.

Here's a normal day in my house:

- Get up and see the kids for a few minutes—literally, less than five—as they are running out of the house to school.
- I work, they go to school and sports activities afterwards.
- Dinnertime—several days a week we make this happen. But sometimes Alec and I are talking about grades or I'm riding Ashley's case about the way she talked to her mother . . . and I ignore Alyssa completely! (Who, very often, won't speak unless spoken to.)
- Homework—they have lots.

- Bedtime. We get ten minutes. If we didn't ask them at dinner, we ask now. "How was your day?" Sometimes that time right before bed is the most we get with them all day.

Add it up! It ain't much.

Lori and I have looked at what we can do to improve on this schedule. Here are a couple things we have tried:

- Breakfast—everyone downstairs by 7 AM so we can spend fifteen minutes together before we all leave for school and work. It actually works sometimes!
- Dinner—we go around the table and all share "highs" and "lows" of the day. This gives everyone a chance to talk—even Alyssa!
- Filling our heads with the truth—we stop and spend fifteen minutes after dinner reading God's Word together and then having everyone share one way they can try to apply what they heard.
- Before bed—we all meet at the couch, pray together, talk about the next day briefly, and say goodnight!

Forget about the studies, never mind the statistics. Let me share with you my own experience: It's amazing how much better our kids are when we put effort into the above areas!

Family time makes a difference. When you create an environment where kids feel heard, understood, and cared for, it makes a world of difference. When we do the opposite—when we're absent—our kids suffer the consequences.

Years ago my friend Kevin handed me a book that challenged me in the area of being a good leader and a good father. To this day I cite it as one of the best books I've ever read. The book is called *Finishing Strong*, by Steve Farrar.[8]

I later met Steve at a speaking event. He was real and personable. We exchanged a few e-mails about parenting and building leaders. I liked what he had to say, so I used his book often for discipling others and even gave the book as gifts to a bunch of my friends.

In 2001, shortly after 9/11, I received a letter from a close friend of mine, Brian, who was my college roommate. Brian was now with the L.A. Police Department. His letter was candid and open.

November 5, 2001

TO THE GODLY MEN IN MY LIFE:

Howdy gentlemen! Just a quick note to tell you that I am thinking about you and praying for you even now. I am reading through a book right now that one of you gave me (thanks Jonathan), *Finishing Strong*, by Dr. Steve Farrar. It has been a great read so far and God is teaching me things all the time.

Since September 11th my work schedule has been a little strange. For a while we were in charge of guarding the bulk of the LAPD's weapons and ammunition 24 hours a day. That has subsided, but other opportunities to make more money have come up. I was listening to all of my friends at work tell me how much overtime they had been working and how much money they were making. . . . I wanted my share. So I took an optional gig at the LA Coliseum during USC games checking all the trucks going into the Coliseum for bombs, etc.

On a typical game day, Saturday (my normal day off), I would spend 13-15 hours there. Alli and Carissa (wife and daughter) were both asleep when I left, and I worked until after 8 PM. . . . Carissa was already asleep. So I made some good money, but I only saw my daughter asleep in her crib. I told myself that I was working for my family so, "it was okay." I had several other games scheduled, and I began to see the sadness in my wife Alli's eyes when I mentioned the work and the money. . . . I did not understand—I was working for her and Carissa . . . wasn't I?

I brought it before the Lord and it was pretty evident that I should not be working that much. All that to tell you this: I have been blessed with special time with my family by giving up that money. [In] Farrar's book that Jonathan sent me, he has this to say about time with our families:

"Don't let the enemy sucker you into working excessive hours to give your kids more things. Your kids don't need more things. They need you. And they want you. The more time that you can spend with them, the more they are going to want to be like you and know the *heavenly Father who made you such a great dad. That's how you lead your kids to Christ.*"[9]

WOW, that just rocks my world!! Thank you all for being such an integral part of who I am and for modeling this concept for me.

I love you all.

–Brian[10]

When I received the letter, with Brian's permission, I posted it on my Web site to encourage men in ministry. Steve Farrar saw the letter and commented:

> Brian captured the dilemma that every husband and father faces day after day, week after week. There is no issue tougher than the family/career issue. On one hand we are called by God to provide for our families, but if we're not careful, long hours can become an addiction that keeps us from dealing with the real issues at home.
>
> I fight this battle and so do you. And sometimes we get pulled into it very gradually. Then one day we realize that we have been sucked away from our family responsibilities. Brian faced that head-on. I have had to face it after getting way overcommitted in the fall of 2001. The ball is in my court and in yours.
>
> I say that we follow the example that Brian has carved out. And unless I miss my guess, your kids will be just as grateful as Brian's.
>
> —Steve[11]

GIVE 'EM WHAT THEY WANT

In my youth culture training workshops, I often begin with a quiz. In the last couple of years, I used this as one of the quiz questions:

"WHAT MAKES YOUNG PEOPLE THE MOST HAPPY?"

Then I give a selection of answers to choose from:

- Spending time with friends
- Spending time with family
- Money
- Popularity
- Spending time with significant other
- Playing sports
- Receiving colorful Christmas sweaters from Aunt Judy

Which answer would you choose?

The answer that I give comes from a 2007 study in which MTV and the Associated Press did a survey of young people between the ages of thirteen and twenty-four (MTV likes to know its target audience). In this survey, one of the questions they asked young people was, "What makes you happy?"

The answer knocked everyone out of their chairs.

In my seminars, participants nearly always choose *spending time with friends* or *spending time with a significant other*. Good guesses. Those actually were the second- and third-most popular answers.

The number one answer? *Spending time with family.*

Are we starting to see a pattern here? When mom and dad show their love by investing time into the family, kids reap the rewards. Better yet, family time isn't loathed by kids; it actually meets a felt need. Seventy-three percent of the 1,280 young people polled said mom and dad make them "happy."

The survey went on to ask this group of young people who their hero was. Twenty-nine percent of students said mom is their "hero"; another 21 percent gave that title to dad. Forget Oprah or Spiderman—half of young people choose mom, dad, or both!

The survey also revealed that only 47 percent of those in this age bracket with divorced parents are "happy" compared with 64 percent of kids who live with both parents. I know this is hard for a lot of us to read. But let's stay candid, Mom and Dad: you need to know that your choices affect your teenagers.[12]

Kids want family. They crave relationships. That's why the top three answers on the above survey were all relationships (family, friends, significant other). If they can't find family at home, they'll look for it somewhere else. I've worked with enough gang members in my day to see that happen—the gang becomes their family.

Even Tom and Tina, the brother and sister I wrote about earlier in this chapter, craved attention from mom and dad. As dad grew more and more aloof, the kids grew skeptical. But if you would have asked them, "Hey Tom," or "Hey Tina: would you rather have a dad who's not around much, not always checking up on you, or a dad who actually cares and shows up?" I guarantee they'd choose a dad who was there for them. No one wishes for a deadbeat dad.

Our kids and teenagers want us in their lives. When we choose to give them what they want—us—we can make a huge impact.

WHEN PARENTS GIVE UP

Sadly, some of the greatest examples of the positive impact we could have are seen when we aren't there. In many of the examples above, we see the choices kids start to make when mom and dad don't respond to their calling as parents.

I hear it all the time from parents:

- "I'm just too busy."
- "I didn't get much attention from my parents when I was their age."
- "They're doing just fine. They'd rather I stay out of their way anyway."

So what happens when parents just give up like this and choose to ignore their kids' desire for family time?

When parents don't step up, others gladly fill in. The first two in line will be the media and peers.

Most of us are familiar with the term "latchkey kids." This became a label for kids who came home to empty homes and used their "latchkey" to open the front door and fend for themselves until mom or dad came home from their busy workday. These empty homes typically allow more "freedom" for kids to "raise themselves."

Mom and dad aren't there for advice, so these kids often turn to the media. How do you resolve conflict? TV provides all the answers you need with *Dr. Phil.* Questions about sex? MTV provides Dr. Drew.

Wanna escape into the world of Hip-hop? Dr. Dre. Philosophy? How about Dr. Seuss? Fulfillment? Dr Pepper. You get the idea.

Parents only have an impact on their kids' lives when they are present and available. Unfortunately, parents aren't always as "present" as they should be. Maybe that's why Walt Mueller, president of the Center for Parent-Youth Understanding (www.cpyu.org) puts the influence of parents third on his list.

In his book *Engaging the Soul of Youth Culture,* Mueller, the noted youth culture expert, a Christian, lists the top four influences on kids today:

1. Media
2. Friends and peers
3. Family
4. School[13]

When I first read his list, I was a little bit bummed out as a parent. And most of the data out there (as you've seen multiple times in this chapter) puts the influence of parents at number one.

Bothered by this, I decided to call my friend Walt. We've done a few podcasts together and we teach at a lot of the same conventions.

When Walt answered, he was on the way to his son's lacrosse game. That's something else I like about Walt. He doesn't just talk about this stuff—he walks it! He invests in his own kids' lives and they'd attest to that.

I asked Walt candidly: "In *Engaging the Soul of the Youth Culture,* you list parents as third in the top four influences. That surprised me a bit." I continued, "Almost everything I read has them as number one. Why do you have them as number three?"

Walt didn't miss a beat. "Jonathan, parents always have the biggest influence if they do what they're supposed to do. The list in my book isn't a list of the way it 'could be'—it's a list of the way it is." You could hear the heartache in his voice. "Unfortunately, parents aren't spending the time they should with their kids and so those other two influences are stepping up and having the most influence."

We talked about that sad reality for a few minutes. He finished with this powerful statement. "It all comes down to whether parents are fulfilling their God-given role or forsaking it. The reason that list looks the way it does is because they're forsaking it."

That's pretty strong. It's up to you.

WHEN WE MADE THE DECISION TO BECOME PARENTS, WE STEPPED INTO A ROLE THAT HAS GREAT RESPONSIBILITY. WE CAN FULFILL THAT ROLE BY GIVING OUR KIDS ONE OF THE MOST PRECIOUS GIFTS WE'LL EVER GIVE THEM—TIME. OR . . . WE CAN FORSAKE THAT ROLE, AND LET LADY GAGA AND EMINEM RAISE OUR KIDS INSTEAD.

It's your choice. A choice that begins with simply being there for your kids. In the next chapter we're going to explore exactly what that looks like. Are you still with me?

• CANDID QUESTIONS FOR REFLECTION •

Some Questions for You, You & Your Spouse, or Your Small Group to Ponder

1. **THIS CHAPTER** began by revealing the enormous amount of time our kids spend absorbing entertainment media each day. How much time does your family spend with these influences?

2. **WHAT OTHER** influences seem to compete for your kids' attention, making it hard for you to make a difference in their lives?

3. **HOW MANY** family dinners do you have in your house each week? What would it take for you to increase the amount of family dinners (or breakfasts)? In what ways could you be more intentional about what is talked about at the kitchen table?

4. **HOW HAVE** you witnessed the effect of parents ignoring their kids? What does that look like?

5. **GO THROUGH** your typical day similar to the way it was laid out in this chapter. How many minutes would you say, on average, that you spend in conversation with your kids? How could you make some changes in that schedule to increase that amount of time?

6. **WALT MUELLER** ranked parents as the third-biggest influence in kids' lives. He said, "This isn't a list of the way it *could be*—it's a list of the way *it is*." What is the current ranking in your house? Why?

7. **TAKE HONEST** inventory: if you're not number one in your kids' lives, what specific things can you do to move toward that goal?

3

BEING THERE

(DISCOVERING QUALITY TIME)

ROB WALKED INTO THE GYMNASIUM where the summer school graduation ceremony was taking place, making his way over to the bleachers . . . where he sat by himself.

Forty-six students received diplomas that day. Not one parent had shown up for the ceremony.

In all honesty, Rob hadn't even planned on going. He just stopped by the empty campus that morning to chat with some of the administration. That's when he heard his name called from across campus. "Rob! I knew you'd come!"

Rob looked across the grassy quad and saw an eighth grader named Brianna running toward him.

Rob knew Brianna from the campus ministry program he led at that school. Rob ministers in one of the most affluent neighborhoods in the area. Much of his time is devoted to building relationships with kids. Rob spends a lot of time on campus, at football games, anywhere that kids hang out—his calendar is packed during the school year. During the summer, activity around campus slows down.

That summer morning, Rob was just running some errands and decided that he'd stop by the campus to make small talk with some administrators. Rob regularly communicates with them, anyone from the ladies at the front office to the school principal.

It was then, when Rob was walking out of the administration building and heading to his car, that he heard Brianna calling his name.

She threw her arms around him and said, "Oh Rob, I knew you'd come—I knew you'd come! We're all graduating today."

Rob, being the man of integrity that he is, did what most people would have done at that moment.

He lied!

"Brianna, I wouldn't have missed it for the world."

Brianna proudly brought him into a room full of what looked like about fifty students and some faculty. He greeted a crowd of smiling students, gave high fives, and then wandered over to the bleachers, the area where parents and extended family were supposed to sit.

This was the graduation for all the summer school kids. Most of these kids hadn't passed one or more of their classes during the year and, by completing summer school, they were now graduating eighth grade and completing middle school. Rob took his seat in the empty bleachers. Not one parent, uncle, cousin, brother, or even grandma was there. Rob cheered, applauding and whistling loudly as forty-six kids received their middle school diplomas.

Brianna came up to Rob afterward with tears in her eyes and said, "Rob . . . you can be my dad anytime!"

Rob came home a different person. The empty room he sat in reflected a perfect picture of our society: empty kids, with empty lives . . . in an empty room.

ONE OF OUR CHIEF ROLES AS A PARENT IS JUST *BEING THERE*. IT'S NOT GOOD ENOUGH TO JUST UNDERSTAND THE FACT THAT PARENTS *CAN* MAKE A DIFFERENCE. WE HAVE TO MAKE A CONSCIOUS DECISION TO ACT ON OUR CONVICTIONS.

We need to make our calendar reflect our belief that parents play a vital role in the lives of our kids. This might start with the simple act of showing up to our son's games or our daughter's plays. Our presence speaks volumes.

Parents have plenty of distractions these days. A 2008 USC survey discovered that 28 percent of Americans admit to spending "less time" than they previously did with members of their households. That was more than double the 11 percent that said the same just two years earlier! TV and the Internet are the two biggest distractions cited by the study.[14] As our society becomes more technologically advanced, we have more gadgets competing for our attention. The *one* piece of technology parents should use more is their digital calendar, carving out time to be there for their kids.

BE THERE OR . . .

It's funny. I don't know how much our kids notice when we're there, but they sure notice when we're not there. Yesterday I went to Alyssa's high school water polo game. We drove across town, pulled two camping chairs out of the trunk of our car, and made our way to the area next to the pool. Lori and I found a spot in partial shade and got as comfortable as we could in a twelve-dollar chair on a cement pool deck.

The guys' team was still playing, so it would be forty-five minutes before Alyssa played. Lori and I have never mastered the art of predicting exactly when Alyssa's game would start. There is no announced starting time; it's always just after the two varsity games—whenever that is!

So we waited for those 45 minutes, excited to hear the final whistle. Our little Lyssy was next. She walked by with a friend and I waved to her.

She waved.

Yeah. That's all I got.

FORTY-FIVE MINUTES IN A CAMPING CHAIR, ONE LEG IN THE SUN, THE OTHER ASLEEP, MY DAUGHTER FINALLY SEES ME . . . AND ALL I GET IS A HAND GESTURE?

Welcome to the world of parenting teenagers.

Two years ago we would have gotten a hug. But with Alyssa—ever since high school—we're happy to get a hand gesture.

A lot of parents might call it in right there. "Forget it. She doesn't even care!"

Trust me. She does.

My friend Rob can attest to that. Forty-six kids received diplomas with no one to take their picture, no one to congratulate them, and no one to say, "I'm proud of you for finishing what you started."

All three of my kids play sports. My dad and mom call Lori and I regularly and ask us, "When is Ashley's soccer game?" "When is Alyssa's match?" Our kids often have their parents *and* their grandparents at their games and events.

Lori is always amazed that my parents show up. She says, "It is so wonderful that your parents come to our kids' events! Did they always come to your events?"

"Yep." I'd think back. "Even sports where I stunk, like swimming. I never won a swim race in my life. But my dad would ask, 'When's your swim meet, Jonathan? I want to make sure and schedule my appointments around it.'"

Lori and I are in a fellowship group at our church with a bunch of parents of teenagers. We get together frequently and talk about these kind of parenting practices—attending our kids' concerts, sports events, and school plays. We often joke about how painful it is to attend some of these events—how grueling all-day swim meets can be, or how seemingly pointless it is to be a spectator at a cross country race where you only see them at one or two quick points along the course and maybe, if you're lucky, at the finish line!

It takes commitment from parents to simply show up at these kinds of activities.

Many of our friends in this group reflect back and share stories of going to their own sports activities as kids and seeing other parents there . . . but not *their* parents. It's not uncommon to see a person tear up when they share something like this from their childhood.

KIDS MIGHT BARELY NOTICE WHEN WE ARE THERE, BUT THEY *REALLY* NOTICE WHEN WE'RE NOT THERE!

CONVERSATION

Parenting styles differ across the board. If you keep your eyes open for articles on parenting, you'll find scholars who will argue for discipline and structure, and experts who swear by a polar opposite methodology, one with lots of freedom and little restraint. I've read compelling research for both sides.

Regardless of their differences, these opposing sides almost unanimously agree on one staple principle of parenting: *being there.*

A month ago (as I write this), three parenting articles/reports came across my desk in one week. The first was from the American Academy of Pediatrics and titled "Sexuality, Contraception, and the Media." This report recommends that parents do three things: recognize the effect of the media, exert control over their kids' media choices, and remove TVs from their kids' bedrooms. It encourages open conversation about media in conjunction with imposing these boundaries.[15]

The second article I saw was from an author who contended just the opposite. She argued that kids will watch what they want anyway—sneaking or watching it at friends' houses. So we might as well let them watch what they want but engage in regular conversations with them about it.

The third report was from a woman named Amy Schalet in the sociology department at the University of Massachusetts Amherst. In her study, "Sex, Love, and Autonomy in the Teenage Sleepover," she compared U.S. parenting styles to those in the Netherlands. The differences in the countries' birthrate percentages were astounding. In 2007, births by American teens (aged fifteen to nineteen) were eight times as high as in the Netherlands. Schalet contends that Dutch parents "normalize" adolescent sexuality—allowing their 16-year-old-daughters to have a boyfriend spend the night, in contrast to typical American parents, who "dramatize" adolescent sexuality. Schalet argues that the Dutch approach basically opens up the communication channels between parents and teenagers about sex and relationships (a rather extreme stance, I realize).[16]

I probably read fifty to a hundred of these kinds of articles and studies every year. Most of the reports I read (especially medical journals/studies from The American Psychological Association, The Kaiser Foundation, The American Academy of Pediatrics, etc.) tend to err on the side of instilling parental boundaries (as opposed to the two latter reports that I just cited). That doesn't mean I ignore the above reports—and it doesn't mean I embrace all their findings. (For instance, the Bible is clear about whether you should consider having your teen daughter host her boyfriend for a sleepover!) But I do look for the kernels of truth or, better yet, common denominators between all the opinions expressed.

Did you notice the common denominator in all three above opinions?

Despite polar opposite parenting styles, all three authors agreed on one thing: *Parents need to regularly engage in conversation with their kids.* Phrases like, "Talk to your kids about this" and "Address these issues!" keep surfacing.

I'm writing this in an airport waiting for a plane. The TV is on next to me—everyone is watching a pro football game. Ironically, as I typed the last paragraph, a commercial came on that said, "Just talk with your kids about drug abuse. Your conversation could make a world of difference!"

Are we listening?

I'm in this airport because I just finished teaching a parenting seminar. After every seminar a line of parents come up to talk with me and ask questions. When they ask questions, I usually come back with a few questions of my own. The first question I ask is almost always, "Are you spending time with your kid?"

Funny, I never have a parent respond, "Yes. Tons! You'd be amazed how much time I spend with my kids!" Instead, parents usually hang their heads a little bit lower and say something like "I try." And then, within seconds, the excuses kick in. "But I'm really busy! . . . I work. . . . The kids have sports. . . . My mother is sick. . . . The dog got its leg stuck in the dishwasher . . ."

News flash: we're all busy, most of us work, our kids always have school and activities, people get sick, our dogs get their legs caught . . . uh . . . well . . . maybe not that last one.

We need to do life with our kids. If we have errands, we should take them with us and stop for ice cream on the way home. If they have sports, *be there* in the bleachers cheering. Engage in conversations to and from practice and games. If we're taking care of an elderly relative, we should involve our kids in the process. Allow them to engage in conversations with grandma or grandpa. Afterward, we can ask them what they thought of the experience. And if the dog gets its leg stuck in the dishwasher . . . yep, involve the kids in getting Max's paw out. See how we can do life with our kids in *every* circumstance?

We need to toss our excuses aside and start connecting with our kids.

MORE THAN JUST PROXIMITY

Building relationships with our kids and teenagers is more than just sitting within five feet of them. Being there is a great start, but all the studies I quoted above instruct us to engage in *conversation* with our kids. How can we really get to know them if we don't dialogue with them about daily life?

In 2004 a California mom learned the hard way that she didn't know her kid as much as she thought she did. Roberta "Bobbi"

MacKinnon died from injuries after being flung from a playground merry-go-round propelled by a rope tied to the back of a vehicle. Bobbi and her friends had watched the show *Jackass* and decided to try to copy their merry-go-round stunt. The result was fatal.

I read about the story in my local newspaper. Joan MacKinnon, Bobbi's mother, said, "I had no idea that she watched the show. Maybe I would have made her stop and think that this is dangerous fun."[17]

I clearly remember my reaction reading Bobbi's mother's words. I swallowed hard and thought: *That could be me! I don't know every show my kids watch. I don't really know their friends very well.*

My kids were young at the time, only six, eight, and ten. When the TV was on, it was usually on cartoons. But in all honesty, I never watched those shows with them. I didn't know exactly who they hung out with at school. *Would my kids have tried this?*

The fact is, many parents don't really know their own kids.

DO YOU KNOW YOUR TEENAGER?

One of the negatives about being a parent and helping with the youth ministry in your own church is knowing things about teenagers that their parents don't know. As a youth worker, I've always dedicated a lot of time to spending one-on-one time with teenagers, mentoring them. This face-to-face time can be pretty revealing. Teenagers will share things that they don't share with their parents.

This is always a tough balancing act. On one hand I want to keep the teenager's trust, but I also feel a responsibility to the parents. If I found out something that the parents needed to know, I would always encourage the teenager to share it with mom and dad. This usually worked. But on occasion, he or she refused to do that. If it was something in which the teenager was in danger, then I told the parents.

The gray areas present the biggest challenges. A teenager is listening to some really raunchy music and the parent has no idea. Is this something I should share? What if she's hanging out with some bad influences? Is this something worth losing her trust to report? These are tough judgment calls that youth workers make daily.

I ALWAYS FIND IT FASCINATING TO NOTE THE DISPARITY BETWEEN WHAT PARENTS *THINK* THEIR TEENAGER IS DOING, AND WHAT THEIR TEENAGER IS ACTUALLY DOING.

One of the biggest areas where we see this great divide is in the area of technology. For example—what teens are doing online compared to what parents *think* they're doing online. I frequently talk with parents who say, "Oh, my little Taylor doesn't do that." But when I talk with Taylor, I quickly discover that he definitely "does that"!

This disparity has reared its head lately in the world of social networking. The great divide between kids' use of social networks and parent's perceptions of the same is propelled largely because many parents are simply unaware of how often teens use these Web sites. Perhaps most telling is the fact that 12 percent of teens with a Facebook and/or MySpace profile admit their parents don't even know about the account's existence. That finding comes from a Common Sense Media report that claims only 23 percent of parents say their child checks an online profile more than once a day when a whopping 51 percent of them do. That's a huge disparity.

Here are some more of their key findings that reveal the staggering disconnect:

- 54 percent of teens admitted to complaining about or making fun of a teacher online, though only 29 percent of parents thought their kids had.
- 39 percent of teens confessed regret over posting something online, while just 20 percent of parents assumed their children would.
- 28 percent of teens shared personal information about themselves that they would not normally share in public, while just 16 percent of their parents thought their kids would.

- 25 percent of teens created a profile for themselves with a different or false identity, but only 12 percent of their parents suspected this.
- 18 percent of teens pretended to be an adult while chatting with someone else online, while only 8 percent of parents thought their teen did this.
- 24 percent of teens admitted they had signed into someone else's social network account or profile without permission, even though a mere 4 percent of parents thought their child was capable of such activity.[18]

TIME TO BE CANDID

Do you know your teenager?

Confession: I found out I didn't know my kids as well as I thought I did.

I'll be the first to tell you that my kids are amazing. I really can't complain. But they will be the first to admit that they've pulled the wool over my eyes numerous times.

I always thought, *There's no way they're gonna outsmart me!* I know! Seriously! I thought that. I've worked with kids so long that I've heard every lie imaginable. Combine that with the fact that I was a really bad kid! I mean it. I snuck out all the time and constantly flew under the radar of adults. As an adult, I recognize a lot of that kind of behavior. (I lived it for many years.)

That said, I've been duped by my kids many times. And I don't just mean little lies. I'm talking about acting one way while living another—for months at a time. I asked Alec if he was comfortable with me sharing an example with you and he told me to tell you the iPod story. In short, over a period of months, Alec downloaded some music onto his iPod from his friend's house. Not only was the music inappropriate, they were illegal downloads (he didn't pay for them). I didn't find out about it until months later. We took his iPod away and had a big talk about trust.

His sisters have pulled some similar moves. Like me, my kids aren't perfect. Any parent who has experienced that kind of situation knows what a heartbreaking event it is the day we discover reality.

I've had some of these experiences happen while I was busy writing articles to parents about how *not* to let it happen. Nothing like a kick in the pants from irony every once in a while to humble you.

How well do you know your kid? Hopefully a little better than the "youth culture expert."

Whenever I do a parent seminar, I like to have parents take a few minutes to fill out a quiz called "Do You Know Your Kid?" I let parents know this quiz isn't a big deal, it won't be graded, and they don't have to turn it in—it's just a way for them to think through how well they know their own kid. So with those guidelines, I tell them to choose one of their kids—no, not *that one*; choose the one you don't know as well—and take the following quiz:

DO YOU KNOW YOUR KID?

1. Who's your kid's best friend?
2. Can you name any of the recent songs/artists that your kid downloaded?
3. What is your kid's favorite movie? TV show?
4. What is your kid's favorite thing to do for fun?
5. Who does your kid like of the opposite gender?
6. Who is your kid's hero?
7. What is your kid passionate about?
8. What are your kid's hopes and dreams for the future?
9. What kind of attention does your kid value from you the most? (Gifts, kind acts, compliments, quality time, conversation, recreational activities . . .)
10. Who does your kid spend the most time talking with online?
11. Have you seen your kid's texting conversations?
12. When is the last time you prayed with your kid?
13. When is the last time you played with your kid?
14. When is the last time you hugged your kid?
15. When is the last time you kissed your kid?

This quiz gets me every time. I make it a point to take the quiz myself whenever I give it to parents. Last weekend (as I write this) I used my son as the object of the quiz.

Alec and I talk quite a bit. We currently go to lunch once a week. (Although, as some of you read this, he'll be away at college. Sniff, sniff.) During these times we regularly dialogue about school, friends, thoughts, feelings . . . life in general.

Let me be honest. Out of an hour-long lunch, it's not like we're spending fifty-two minutes talking about those deep things. We're guys! Much of the conversation is "Dude, these wings rock!" "So good!" "Hey, did you see that there's a new M. Night Shyamalan film coming out?" "Who would win in a fight between Yoda and Gandalf?" (OK, we're not just guys, we're nerds!) But in between licking wing sauce off our fingers and brainstorming movie hypotheticals, we also touch on real life for about ten of those minutes.

But in those ten minutes a week, I learn a little about his friends, any girls of interest, his frustrations, fears, and his relationship with God. I get to know my son!

YOU'D THINK THAT I'D DO PRETTY WELL ON THIS QUIZ THEN, HUH? (AFTER ALL, I WROTE THE STUPID THING!) BUT AS I LOOK AT IT NOW, THERE ARE MORE THAN A FEW QUESTIONS THAT I DON'T KNOW THE ANSWER TO.

After parents take the quiz in the seminar, I tell them: "This isn't a list that you bring with you to your kid's room and start reading them questions like a parole officer. The content of this quiz isn't magical. Once you know this information, your job as a parent isn't done. In fact, the purpose of this quiz is to help most of us realize, *Dang, I don't know my kids as much as I thought I did. I really need to spend some time dialoguing with them.*"

MAKING QUALITY TIME

Wouldn't it be nice if we could just carve out a little bit of time each week for some quality time with our kids? If you're like me, you want to be efficient. Forget the silly talk; let's schedule some time each week for deep conversations where we can talk about deep, meaningful things—quality time!

Most of us have experienced these moments as parents. We're putting our daughter to bed, and she looks up at us and asks, "Mom, when you were my age, did you ever like a boy, but he didn't like you back?" And there it is. You have an amazing conversation where she shares her heart, you share some stories about your past, and she listens. It's a Kodak moment, in words. Sheer quality time.

If you've experienced these wonderful moments, then you probably sailed out of your kid's bedroom that night feeling as if you're on cloud nine. Those are the moments that make parenting worthwhile.

So what do we do? We try to duplicate those moments. Next time you're putting your daughter to bed, you ask her, "Do you have anything you want to ask me?" And she looks in your eyes and says, "Why would I ask you something?"

QUALITY TIME HAS LEFT THE BUILDING.

That's the crazy thing about quality time—you never know when it will happen.

Take those lunches with my son: sometimes it takes several lunches, hours at a time, to get just ten minutes of quality time. That's the thing about quality time. It requires *quantity time.*

As wonderful as it is to experience those deep moments where our kids share their hearts and actually listen to us, those moments don't come often. Moreover, they come when we're willing to invest in other moments with them: silly moments, nurturing moments, adventurous moments . . . doing things they want to do.

One of the quiz questions that I ask of parents that got me was: "When was the last time you played with your kid?" Alec recently asked me, "Dad, do you want to play Xbox?"

I was tired and cranky, so I said, "Not now, buddy. Sorry." He's asked me a few times lately. And to be honest, I'm lame at Xbox. The controller is made for this young, multitasking generation (twentysomethings have no problem with it). I grew up with a joystick. Simple! Move the stick, hit the button. Rotate ship, blow away asteroids!

So Alec has played by himself the last few times he asked me.

What a wasted opportunity!

Who cares if I'm no good! My son asked me to play with him! He's going to be gone in less than a year and I'm going to have flashbacks of me rejecting him—and those flashbacks will come to me in slow motion!

At a Promise Keepers convention, I heard Howard Hendricks, an amazing speaker, say, "Any dad who spends five minutes a day rolling on the floor with his kids—I vote as father of the year." Wow. That's not a real tough standard, if you think about it. How hard is it to just roll on the floor with your kids for five minutes?

We all remember when our kids were young. I remember when I would walk in the door from work and my kids would charge me, grab my legs, and yell, "Daddy's home! Daddy's home!" It was at that moment that I had a choice:

    a) "Kids, not now! I just got home from work and I'm tired!"
    b) Dive on the floor with them and roll for five minutes!

How hard is it to do the latter?

AS OUR TEENAGERS GET OLDER, "ROLLING ON THE FLOOR" TURNS INTO "PLAYING XBOX" OR "PAINTING NAILS." DON'T MISS THESE OPPORTUNITIES.

A regular investment of these small, seemingly inconsequential relational activities paves the way to quality moments.

The trick is the part about a *regular* investment. It takes quantity to get quality. Remember that report from Columbia University ("The Importance of Family Dinners") that I cited in the last chapter? It revealed the numerous drug and alcohol risks that kids who have "infrequent family dinners" face. Do you remember how they defined "infrequent"?

Fewer than three per week.

Think about that for a second. How many families have more family meals together than that?

Something I didn't mention in the last chapter: the report also defined "frequent family dinners." In their comparison of teenagers who have frequent family dinners to those who have infrequent family dinners, they put a number to "frequent family dinners." Got a guess?

Columbia defines it as five to seven per week.

Think about what that might look like in your house. Sunday afternoon—yes; Monday night—doable; forget Tuesday—you have to work late; forget Wednesday—church; Thursday night—sure, but it will be late; forget Friday—kids are always out with friends; and . . . squeeze in a breakfast on Saturday? Does this sound something like your house?

That's only four family dinners! Five to seven is no joke. That's some serious quantity time.

Make it happen. I'm not saying that family dinners are magical. But what I'm saying—and what those who did the Columbia University report would argue—is that the more time a family spends together laughing, talking, and doing life together, the more chance that those kids will bond with their parents and avoid the trouble that kids without those bonds seem to gravitate toward.

It starts with quantity time. Quantity time with our kids and teenagers builds relational bonds. Our kids—whether three or twenty-three—are going to open up with the people that they trust and feel close to. If we don't invest in a relationship with them, then they won't be as eager to share their heart with us. Roll with them on the floor for five minutes now . . . and maybe they'll open up and ask you those deep questions later.

It takes quantity time to get quality time.

RULES WITHOUT A RELATIONSHIP

Ashley plays soccer and has practice two to three days a week. Two coaches are there every time I drop Ashley off at practice. I've probably seen them there thirty or forty times. They're there for every game too.

One Saturday I saw this other guy standing at the sideline with the other two coaches, hollering at the kids. The kids weren't responding to this man at all. I'm out of town about six days a month, so I figured that I had missed the introduction to him. I asked Lori, "Who's the new guy?"

"He's one of the assistant coaches."

I was confused. I turned to her and lowered my voice. "I've never seen him . . . ever."

She leaned in close to me. "I know. I've only seen him twice now."

He kept barking orders at the girls, and they all kept looking at him like, *Who the heck are you?*

A couple of weeks later, pictures came out. Ashley opened them up, took one look and started on a tirade. "I can't believe this guy's in the picture!"

I looked at the picture. This "ghost coach" was standing on the side in clear view of everyone, while one of the dedicated coaches was humbly tucked behind, peeking over the heads of the girls.

Ashley ranted and pointed to the man whose name I still don't know. "Why is *he* standing there like he's all that and we can't even see Coach Scott!" (It was pretty funny.)

To Ashley and the other girls on the team, this man had not earned their respect. And when he barked orders to them, most of them didn't even listen.

It's been said so often that I don't even know who to credit: "Rules without a relationship leads to rebellion."

Some of us have experienced this as parents. We work all day, neglect our kids at night, barely see them on the weekends . . . and then we start barking some orders toward them at random. They look at us like, *Who the heck are you? Keep barking Mr.-never-here-don't-care-sit-in-my-chair-and-read-the-paper-and-ignore-the-kids!!!*

We can't expect our kids to listen to us, take correction from us, and take our instructions when we're not even willing to listen to them.

Be there. Have conversations with them. Spend quantity time, opening the door to quality time.

So what if conversations don't come easily? I've said it numerous times in this chapter: *be there.* Maybe you're convinced of this. You're willing to be there, you're even willing to give quantity time to try to harness a few minutes of quality conversation . . . but you may still be wondering, *What's the first step?*

It all starts with finding communication arenas. That's what we're going to spend the next chapter talking about.

• CANDID QUESTIONS FOR REFLECTION •

Some Questions for You, You & Your Spouse, or Your Small Group to Ponder

1. **WHAT ARE** some of the distractions that keep you from *being there*?

2. **NAME A** time when you tried to initiate conversation with your kid(s) and got shut down. Why do you think this happened?

3. **SEVERAL STUDIES** were cited that revealed disparity between what parents believed about their kids and the reality of the situation. What is an area of your kids' lives where you might guess that they act differently than you think?

4. **REVIEW THE** "Do You Know Your Kid?" quiz. Which questions were tough ones for you? For a few of those, tell why.

5. **SHARE A** quality time moment you've had with your kid(s). What was it about the timing and the environment that helped them feel comfortable enough to open up?

6. **WHAT ARE** some ways in which you can increase quantity time with your kids so you can know them better (and thus maybe get a higher score on the "Know Your Kid" quiz!)?

7. **WHAT ADJUSTMENTS** do you need to make to your schedule this week to get more family dinners or create other "arenas" of quality time?

HOT TUBS AND NAIL SALONS

(ARENAS WHERE COMMUNICATION IS CULTIVATED)

WHEN MY BROTHER AND I were fourteen and fifteen, my dad made a purchase that revolutionized communication in our house.

He bought a hot tub.

It's amusing how this purchase came about. Our neighbor was moving and asked if we wanted her hot tub. She couldn't take it to her new house, and the people buying her old house didn't want it. So she asked my dad, "You want a free hot tub? You can have the wood decking around it too."

It took my dad two seconds to think about this. "Yep!" was his reply.

The next day my dad, my brother, and I were at the neighbor's house carefully disassembling the wood decking. Eight hours later we had the deck reassembled in our backyard. At that point we quickly became savvy as to why the new homeowners didn't want the old tub. Even though the decking was nice, this "free hot tub" was a piece of junk. It not only didn't work, it was covered in mold and stains.

Next, my dad did something that I never saw my parents do—ever! He made a spontaneous purchase. He went out that day and bought a new hot tub to fit into our newly installed decking. (Maybe he just didn't want a deck with a huge hole in it.)

A week later our family was sitting in our brand new hot tub looking up at the stars.

This became a regular practice before bedtime. My dad didn't want to go out in the hot tub alone, so about thirty minutes before our bedtime he would propose, "If you want to go to bed, you can . . . or you can stay up and go in the hot tub with me."

Yeah. Hot tub won over bedtime every night.

And that's when it happened.

We started opening up and communicating.

My dad looks back at that purchase as one of the best he's ever made. To this day he will tell us, "Before we bought the hot tub, deep conversations were sparse. But once we began our evening hot tub excursions, you guys couldn't stop talking. We'd get out under the stars and you'd each bare your soul."

My dad still ponders the situation. "At the time I probably thought the reason you talked so much was because I was such a good listener. But now that I reflect on the situation, I think it was just because you didn't want to go to bed!"

MY BROTHER AND MY DAD WOULD AGREE WITH ME; THERE WAS NOTHING MAGICAL ABOUT THAT HOT TUB. SURE, IT WAS FUN. AND IT DEFINITELY BEAT GOING TO BED. BUT THE REALITY OF THE SITUATION WAS THE HOT TUB WAS SIMPLY AN ARENA WHERE COMMUNICATION WAS ABLE TO FREELY FLOW.

A hot tub might do the same for you. It might not. But as parents we need to keep our eyes open for these arenas.

WHAT'S YOUR ARENA?

My friend Troy loves riding dirt bikes. He has great memories of his father teaching him how to ride a motorcycle off-road for the first time. As Troy grew up, dirt bikes became a regular part of family vacations. They rode as a family and competed on weekends.

When Troy started a family of his own, the motocross legacy was passed on. Troy bought quads for his kids when they were young. Soon he purchased a huge fifth wheel toy-hauler that slept seven and carried all the family bikes. With toys like these, motocross camping weekends became a staple activity.

Something happened on these frequent trips with the entire family. Troy and his kids began bonding. Four people in one vehicle for hours at a time leads to conversation (and a few squabbles). Riding through the woods together, fixing broken quads on the top of a sand dune together, roasting marshmallows over a fire after a long day of riding . . . these are all fun memories for Troy, his wife, and their kids. And motocross camping trips became their primary arena of communication. His family is as tight-knit as they come.

My friend Eric put in a swimming pool. One night I was talking to him about our favorite movies and TV shows. I'll never forget what Eric said. He shrugged his shoulders and told me, "Jonathan, we don't watch many movies or much TV. Our family just hangs out by the pool."

Eric's pool has been his family's arena of communication.

My friend Lorin has a ski boat. Yep—an arena of communication. The sky's the limit.

At this point you might be thinking: *Jonathan, all those examples are great, but many of them are also expensive. Are all arenas of communication so expensive?*

Great question.

When I was little, my dad started taking me to breakfast once a week. I'll never forget it. We lived in Southern Illinois, and there was a big Holiday Inn hotel near our house. I didn't even know what the restaurant was called; it was just this little breakfast place inside the hotel.

My dad would take me to breakfast every Tuesday morning and we'd talk. He'd ask me about my week and listen to me. In retrospect, these conversations probably weren't very deep. But to me, a seven-year-old, they meant the world. My dad was interested in me. He and I had that special time. No one could take that away from me. I valued that time.

I still don't know the name of that place, but it was an arena of communication. It was *our* place to communicate, to just hang out and talk. And it cost my dad less than $10 a week.

Like my friend Troy, I decided to pass down my heritage. Unfortunately, my heritage didn't involve dirt bikes. Or maybe I should say, *fortunately* for my budget and my health, my heritage didn't involve dirt bikes. It only required breakfasts. So a few years ago, I began taking my kids to breakfast. I took my son, the oldest one, once a week, and I alternated my daughters each week. (I figured, when my son was gone from the house, I'd get more time with my girls.)

We have a little greasy spoon diner near my house that had $1.99 breakfasts. I know! Amazing. (Those breakfasts are $2.49 now. . . . Still amazing!) All this was nice on the budget. For two of us, breakfast cost me all of four bucks, plus tax and tip. (Although we usually had to bring a flyswatter.)

That greasy little diner was an arena of communication.

As parents, we need to constantly be on the lookout for arenas where communication is cultivated.

If you have no idea what type of arena would work with your

COMMUNICATION ARENA IDEAS

- Shopping for clothes
- Eating hot wings at a sports bar
- Talk during your commute to school
- Bedside conversations at bedtime
- Hiking
- Baking a favorite dessert
- Fishing
- Lounging in an overstuffed couch at a coffee bar while sipping mochas
- RV'ing
- Hot tubs!
- The corner booth at a greasy diner eating French fries
- Manicures, pedicures, makeovers
- Sharing an oversized ice cream sundae
- Lying on lounge chairs by a swimming pool
- Floating down the river in kayaks
- Riding on a tandem bicycle
- Lunch dates at *their* favorite place

own kid, then simply observe them. Observe their interests. Does your son like food (seriously, what growing boy can't eat *ALL THE TIME*?)? What kind of food? What is his favorite restaurant? How would he respond if you said, "Josh! Let's go get some onion rings!"

Does your daughter like getting her nails done? What would she say if you told her, "Megan, let's go get a pedicure."

Do any of your kids like animals? What if you said to one of them, "Morgan, let's go to the pet store at the mall and hold kittens."

AFTER TWENTY MINUTES OF EATING GREASY ONION RINGS, OR WHILE THE NAIL POLISH IS DRYING, OR AFTER YOU'VE EACH NAMED YOUR FAVORITE KITTEN . . . YOU MIGHT JUST FIND YOUR KID BEGINNING TO OPEN UP.

DOOR-OPENING QUESTIONS

It doesn't hurt to give communication a little nudge every once in a while. You can do this by asking good questions. Nothing too deep. Nothing difficult to answer. Instead, ask a fun question that your kid would want to answer.

> *What's your favorite place to get onion rings?*
> *Would you rather have a manicure, pedicure, or a massage?*
> *What would you name this kitten with the three legs? Tripod? Gimpy?*

Ask light questions in the area of their interest. If you're eating onion rings, a question about onion rings might be just the thing.

You can call these light and fun questions icebreakers. Here's a bunch of good ones:

> *What's your favorite restaurant and what would you order if we were there right now?*
> *If you could make a playlist with your favorite songs on it, what five songs would be on the list?*

If you could travel anywhere in the world on a one-week vacation, where would you go? Who would you take with you?
If you could tame any animal as a pet, what animal would you tame?
If someone offered to buy you any car that you wanted, but you had to pay for the gas and the insurance . . . what car would you get?
What is your dream date? Who would it be with?

Think about the insight you'll gain from some of these questions. *Five favorite songs?* If they name some crude artists, don't overreact. Just store that information for a later conversation. (I'll talk more about this in chapter 6, "Dad, Can I Download This Song?") *Who would you bring with you on a one-week vacation?* Now you're learning who their best friends are. *Dream date?* You'll discover their romantic interests. All of these questions are nonthreatening, but the answers can be content-rich.

Some light and fun icebreakers can lead to deeper questions. Here are a few examples of light questions that can segue into deeper conversations:

If you could have any super power, what power would you want? What would you do with it?
What's the best day you ever had? What's the worst day you ever had?
If you had $100 to spend at any one store, what store would you go to and what would you buy?
If you had $100 to spend on someone else, who would you spend it on, and what would you buy?
What was your high point of the day? week? What was your low point of the day? week?

MORE ICEBREAKER QUESTIONS

- What are your favorite pizza toppings?
- Tell me something about the clothes (or shoes) you're wearing.
- If you were at your favorite ice cream shop and it had every flavor in the world, what flavor would you get?
- What was your favorite cartoon when you were little?
- If you could only watch one TV show, what would it be?
- What's your favorite season? Why?
- What's your favorite sport to play?
- What's your favorite sport to watch?
- What's your favorite holiday?
- If you could get one day off school, what would you do with it?
- What chore do you hate the most?
- If you had to die your hair one color of the rainbow, what color would it be?
- What's something you'd like to eat some day?
- Would you rather drive on vacation, fly, or take a train?

You can also ask icebreaker questions that are fun and deep at the same time.

> *If you could make one wish and you knew it would come true, what would you wish for?*
> *What is one quality you wish you had, but probably never will, just because of the way God made you?*
> *What is one attainable quality you could have, but would take a lot of work to get? What would you have to do to get it?*

The goal is to get them talking.

MORE DOOR-OPENING QUESTIONS

- If they made a movie of your life, who would you want to play you?
- Would the movie be a comedy, a romantic comedy, a drama, or an action film?
- What job would you like to do when you grow up? What do you think it's going to take for you to get there?
- What's the greatest song ever written?
- What was your most embarrassing moment ever?
- If you could meet one celebrity, who would you want to meet?
- If you could ask God one question, what would you ask him?
- Who is your hero?
- Who is someone you know only a little who you'd like to get to know deeper?
- If you could go back and change one choice you've made, what would you change?
- What's something I can pray about for you?

LET'S STOP AND THINK ABOUT THIS FOR A MOMENT. THE GOAL IS TO GET *THEM* TO TALK. THE GOAL ISN'T TO SIT THEM DOWN AND LECTURE THEM.

In the youth ministry world I see leaders make this mistake far too often. They meet kids and the first thing they do is try to get them to sit down and listen to their long speeches. What a lost opportunity. Think how much better it is when our kids are welcomed to a secure place where they feel *heard*.

As parents, we want to create an arena where our kids feel safe to open up and share things with us. Their favorite onion rings place might lead to them sharing their highs and lows of the week. You might ask more about the vulnerable "low" they just shared. You may not have to say much. The floodgates could open as soon as they realize that you're there to *really* listen. And, if they think you've never done that before, be prepared to see the shock on their face.

My daughter Alyssa isn't as verbal as my other two. If Lori or I ask Alyssa how her day at school was, the answer will be, "Fine." Not another word. In contrast, if I ask my other two children the same question, I'll get a play-by-play of the entire day.

If Alyssa is depressed about something and I ask her what's wrong, I guarantee she'll answer, "Nothing." Then total silence.

Alyssa is a little bit like an old car. She needs to be warmed up before she gets going.

So with Alyssa, I've learned to never ask questions that can be answered with one word. Instead of asking, "How was your day?" I ask, "What was the best part of your day today?"

I do this a lot with Alyssa:

> *If you could do anything this weekend, what would you want to do?*
> *Show me your favorite outfit! (Alyssa loves clothes right now.)*
> *How would you redesign your room if you could redo it*
> *this weekend?*

Alyssa takes some nurturing before she starts talking. Each kid has his or her own language. Alyssa likes corny humor, so I'll use that with her.

"Did your hamster die?" (She doesn't have a hamster.)

"No."

"Dog die?" (We *do* have a dog.)

She plays along. "I don't know. Did he?"

I call the dog. He runs in the room wagging his bushy little mutant tail. Our dog is supposed to have a straight tail, but he has a curly, fuzzy little tail. We don't know why. He's just a mutant.

"Nope," I pronounce. "He's still alive. See. You can see him wagging his little mutant tail. He's alive."

"Dang," she'll say, cracking a smile.

I'll ask Alyssa a couple more questions about things she's interested in to warm her up, and finally she'll start to open up. When she does . . . *I listen.*

Our kids will be more likely to talk to us if they know that we're there to listen.

Consider how great it would be if our kids felt like they could communicate with us and be heard.

We need to create arenas where communication is cultivated. We need to be ready to ask questions. We need to be ready to listen.

EVERYONE SHOULD BE QUICK TO LISTEN, SLOW TO SPEAK AND SLOW TO BECOME ANGRY (JAMES 1:19).

As communication is nourished and starts to grow, your relationship with your kid will grow. Trust will develop.

Sometimes it takes effort to find these arenas with our kids. For a time, Lori was struggling to find an arena of communication with Alyssa. Alyssa has a black belt in one-word answers. Lori would try the same approach I tried and Alyssa wouldn't open up.

Then one day Alyssa needed some shoes. Lori took her shopping.

Boom. It happened. Take Alyssa shoe shopping and she lights up like a Christmas tree. The two of them came home from the mall laughing and talking. That was the funny thing. The conversation continued for the rest of the evening. Lori opened the gateway of communication with Alyssa, and it kept flowing until bedtime.

Now if Lori needs some Alyssa time . . . it's *off to the mall!* They don't even have to spend that much money. They window shop, talk about what outfits are cutest, and then stop by the See's Candy counter and get a few pieces of the most delicious chocolate on the West Coast.

Now the two of them wear almost the exact same size, so they have a vested interest in what the other buys. You guessed it: they borrow each other's clothes on a weekly basis.

Shoes, clothes, the mall: arenas of communication.

THE LONG HAUL

Communication is like a garden. If you cultivate it and work at it, it will grow and produce great fruit.

ONCE COMMUNICATION IS FLOWING, DON'T GIVE UP ON THE CULTIVATION. IF YOU ABANDON A GARDEN, CROPS WILL DIE AND WEEDS WILL GROW.

Similarly, don't make the mistake of discovering an arena of communication only to abandon it after a few runs.

I once taught a parenting seminar in a small town in Kentucky. During the seminar I told the story about my dad's hot tub. I encouraged the parents at that workshop to find an arena of communication with their kids.

The next day I spoke to the teenagers at the same church. After my talk two girls walked up. One pointed her finger at me enthusiastically and proclaimed, "You're awesome! My parents want to buy a hot tub because of you!"

Her friend looked at her and asked, "Why?"

The excited girl told her friend, "He told a story to our parents yesterday about when his dad bought a hot tub. It helped them communicate better. So my mom is going to buy a hot tub!"

Her friend asked, "So your parents went to a workshop yesterday?"

Hot tub girl replied, "Yeah." She rolled her eyes. "They have all these ideas now."

Her friend then said something I'll never forget: "Don't worry. My parents went to one of those seminars a few years ago, too, and got a bunch of ideas." She patted her friend on the shoulder and assured her, "It won't last."

What a sad stigma to leave behind as your parenting legacy.

Don't let your finding an effective arena of communication be a temporary gesture.

Find places where communication is cultivated—and make it an *ongoing* process.

• CANDID QUESTIONS FOR REFLECTION •

Some Questions for You, You & Your Spouse, or Your Small Group to Ponder

1. **WHAT SPECIFIC** (where and when) communication arenas have you already discovered that work for your kids?

2. **WHAT EXAMPLES** of communication arenas mentioned in this chapter sparked interest, or seem worth a try with your kids?

3. **IN THE** next week, what are some ways you'll intentionally plan a few of these activities that might open up great conversations with your kids? (For instance: How are you going to go about asking your daughter out on a date?)

4. **HOW WILL** you *make sure you keep the momentum for these meetings going so that they don't fade away?*

5. **WHICH ICEBREAKER** or door-opening questions mentioned in this chapter do you think your kids would respond to? Where could you take those conversations?

6. **WHAT ARE** some icebreaker or door-opening questions you can think of that your kids will respond to? Where could you take those conversations?

7. **DO YOU** tend to *listen* or *lecture* when talking with your kids? Why is that? How can you do better at listening and making them feel *heard*?

TEACHING VALUES

5

RAISING THE BAR

(TEACHING OUR KIDS LASTING VALUES)

"MY KID IS GOING TO do it anyway . . . might as well let him drink at home."

How's that for high expectations and strong guidance?

This pessimistic and enabling perspective isn't as rare as you might think. I've heard it from numerous parents—even in the church.

After decade-long declines, drug and alcohol use among high school students spiked in 2009. In 2008 "only" 35 percent of ninth-to-twelfth graders surveyed drank alcohol in the thirty days prior to when they answered the survey. In 2009 the number jumped to 39 percent. In the same twelve months, marijuana use jumped from 32 percent to 38 percent, and the use of the synthetic drug ecstasy jumped from 6 percent to 10 percent.[19]

Robyn Vanover, coordinator of Martin County's (Florida) Safe and Drug Free Schools program, is one educator who has watched this trend. After noticing a similar shifting in her county's 2008 Florida Youth Substance Abuse Survey, she said the spike could be attributed to the low expectations of parents.

Many parents are giving up and letting their kids do what-ever they want. These low expectations give kids permission to try at-risk behaviors, rendering them susceptible to drugs and alcohol.

It doesn't have to be this way!

Vanover said that knowledgeable, engaged, attentive, and communicative parents can make a huge difference. She believes that parents need to set the bar high. "The number one reason kids give as to why they don't use drugs and alcohol is 'my parents,'" Vanover said. "The main reason is always, 'My parents have an expectation of me.'"[20]

Where do you set the bar?

I admit, it's hard to set the bar high today when everyone else keeps knocking it down. The world's standards are stooping pretty low today. The days of Roy Rogers as a hero are dead and gone.

TODAY'S HEROES ARE STEROID-SHOOTING ATHLETES, POT-SMOKING RAPPERS, AND PANTYLESS CELEBRITIES.

It's hard to set a standard when it seems that every other voice around us is preaching the opposite.

Last fall my wife and I chaperoned a public high school dance. Throughout the night, the teachers and administration were walking around trying to enforce a "no dirty dancing policy." This was truly hilarious to watch because the administration was sending mixed messages with its song choices.

Here's how it worked.

The school has a "no explicit songs" policy. That means the DJ played the "clean versions" of all the songs. But, have you *heard* the "clean versions" of songs today? I assure you, "clean version" only means that they have removed the really bad swear words. The message of the song is still very clear.

At this particular dance, the teachers were walking around with flashlights trying to keep the girls from "getting low"—this is where girls start squatting down low, often hiking their skirts up even higher than they already are. I'm not exaggerating when I tell you that the teachers, my wife, and I kept seeing girls' underwear peeking out from underneath their already short skirts throughout the entire dance.

The chaperones were also busy trying to keep the girls from "backing up." Yes, this is another new trend in the last five years. The majority of today's teenagers don't even face each other at a dance. The girl simply turns around and backs into the guy, the guy puts his hands on the girl's hips, and the grinding begins. (I use the word "grinding" because it's really hard to come up with a phrase that means "sex with clothes on.") Sometimes two girls will face each other, almost pressing against one another, and then a guy will appear on each side from behind, sandwiching the girls in the middle.

There was no flashlight that would stop what was going on in that gymnasium. The only thing that would have stopped the "grinding" at that dance was turning off the music and turning on the lights.

Here's the amusing part. While the chaperones were walking around saying, "Stop getting low," or "Stop backing up and wiggling!" the DJ was playing songs like "Get Low" by rappers Lil John & the East Side Boyz. Here's one snippet of the lyrics:

Get low . . . Drop dat body . . .

I encourage you to do a simple Google search of the words "Get Low lyrics" and read the regular version that teenagers know so well.

As you can see from the lyrics, chaperones were saying, "Stop getting low!" while the song said, "Get low." Then the chaperones would say, "Stop backing it up and wiggling against that guy's crotch!" And the song would say, "back it up . . . den wiggle with ya."

What kind of messages are we sending to our teenagers?

"Hey! Stop doing what the songs we are playing for you are telling you to do!"

These kind of mixed messages are commonplace today. Our kids will watch a prime time sitcom on TV where actor Charlie Sheen jumps from bed to bed with different girls, and then a commercial will air about being responsible with sex.

A RAPPER WILL WIN AN AWARD FOR HIS SONG ABOUT ORAL SEX AND THEN HE'LL THANK GOD AND HIS MOM IN HIS ACCEPTANCE SPEECH.

Huh?

It's obvious that our kids aren't going to learn morals and values from the world. It's up to us to teach them lasting values.

What values are we going to pass on to our kids?

WHEN I GROW UP

When you were a kid, what did you want to be when you grew up?

A fireman?

An astronaut?

My friend David R. Smith worked with me at The Source for Youth Ministry for several years. During that time we collaborated on developing parenting resources, and each of us taught parenting seminars across the country. I once heard David ask this question to a group of about sixty parents in a parent workshop he taught: "What did you want to be when you grew up?"

He collected answers from around the room, some humorous, some serious.

"A cop," someone yelled from the back.

"A garbage man!" a man in the front suggested. Laughter erupted around the room. "Seriously!" the man defended. "I did wanna be a garbage man. I wanted to drive that truck with the big mechanical arm that grabbed cans and dumped them in the truck. Those are cool!"

"I always liked helping people," another parent replied. "I wanted to be a nurse."

After about five or six answers, David would gently say: "That's funny. None of you actually answered the question I asked. Each of you answered 'What did you want to *do* when you grew up?' instead of 'What did you want to *be* when you grew up?'"

The room grew quiet.

David continued. "Why didn't any of us answer 'godly,' 'filled with integrity,' 'loving,' or 'Christlike'? To be fair, almost every single one of us would make that mistake. We wrap so much of ourselves into what we *do*—or how we make our money. But let's not confuse *doing* with *being*."

That little exercise really impacted me. We often get so caught up in temporary things like money, status, and power. Our society values external characteristics. How often do we think about internal characteristics?

When David asked people what they wanted to *be*, no one said "a loving husband" . . . "a woman of God" . . . "a man of integrity." Why? Maybe because real values just aren't *valued* by our society today.

VALUES? WHAT VALUES?

Words like "values" or "character" are almost extinct in our popular culture. I bet you could watch TV all day long and not hear either of those words. Instead you'll hear phrases like "lose weight," "look better," and "full head of hair."

> **YOU'LL SEE HOW** PERFECT YOU CAN LOOK IF YOU WHITEN YOUR TEETH WITH ONE BRAND OF PRODUCT AND SHAMPOO YOUR HAIR WITH ANOTHER. DRIVE THE OPPOSITE SEX WILD BY SPLASHING A LITTLE BIT OF SOMETHING ELSE ON YOUR NECK.

Funny. Nothing about honesty or integrity. I guess those aren't important.

Let's be honest. When it's time for a makeover, outward appearance always trumps inward character. A good-looking cheater is much more popular than a moral, funny-looking guy!

Today's American dream includes a big house (no white picket fence necessary, just a huge back patio with a built-in barbecue), a new car in the driveway, and a flat panel in the den. As for the couple living there, marriage is optional, as long as he is tan with perfect abs and she is sufficiently thin, maybe even borderline anorexic, which makes her silicone implants look even bigger.

We're quick to drop big wads of cash for all of the above, but what have we invested in character? How much has the average person spent on "values" this year?

It's a funny thing to consider, because if you think about it, where can you even purchase cosmetics for your inner being? When's the last time you saw a seminar with the title, "Learn how to be honest and pay your fair share of taxes"? Or how about the all-day workshop, "Keep your commitments, including still paying into your upside-down mortgage!" Not very popular seminars.

The fact is, the American dream values temporary thrills, success, and status. Our world doesn't value honesty or honor when they get in the way of fulfillment or accomplishment. If our job is on the line, we're quick to sacrifice family time. Money is more important than values.

This is even reflected in small, daily decisions.

"Four movie tickets for the nine o'clock showing—two tickets for adults and two for children."

"How old are your kids?"

"They're under twelve, ma'am. Both of them."

"But that kid has a beard!"

"He's an early bloomer."

When integrity costs us an extra four bucks a kid . . . who needs honesty?!

In a message about character, I heard this from Andy Stanley, pastor at North Point Community Church (Alpharetta, Georgia): "Whenever character takes a back seat to fulfillment or accomplishment, ethics change. Morality changes. Everything changes."

He nailed it. And our society reflects it.

I remember watching the classic Will Smith film *Independence Day* with my kids. You may have seen it—everyone wakes up to big flying saucers hovering all over the planet and Will Smith's character, Captain Steven Hiller, eventually saves the world. But before we know it, the aliens are destroying New York, L.A., Washington DC, and other major cities all over the world. In the aftermath of the destruction, Captain Hiller's stripper girlfriend Jasmine is trying to reconnect with him. In her journey, she begins to pick up travelers who've been hurt by the blast. One of the people she finds is the first lady of the United States.

In a conversation between the two women, the first lady asks, "So what do you do for a living?"

"I'm a dancer," Jasmine responds.

The first lady smiles in approval. "Ballet."

"Exotic," Jasmine replies, chin held high.

The first lady awkwardly pauses. "Oh, sorry."

"Don't be," Jasmine quickly retorts. "I'm not, it's good money." She rubs the head of her son. "Besides, my baby's worth it!"[21]

American values at their best. *Whenever character takes a back seat to fulfillment or accomplishment, ethics change.* Stripping is OK when it means feeding our kids, right? Was waiting tables at the local diner *not* an option? I guess every pretty waitress in the world just lacks good business sense, because pole dancing pays the bills better, right?

Honesty, integrity, and character—sadly, few places will teach our kids these values. If our kids get a good football coach, he might teach values like commitment and follow-through. If we bring them to church any given week, they might hear about honesty. If they attend a 12-step program, they might learn self-discipline. But how can twelve people sitting in a circle in the basement of a church for an hour once a week compete with more than ten hours of entertainment media daily communicating something else?

Enter parents, stage right.

PASS IT ON

Parents have to teach their kids values. It's their responsibility. It always has been. Look at Deuteronomy chapter 6. Any Jew or Christian would agree that this passage spells out one of the parents' primary responsibilities:

> These are the commands, decrees and laws the Lord your God directed me to teach you to observe in the land that you are crossing the Jordan to possess, so that you, your children and their children after them may fear the Lord your God as long as you live by keeping all his decrees and commands that I give you, and so that you may enjoy long life. Hear, O Israel, and be careful to obey so that it may go well with you and that you may increase greatly in a land flowing with milk and honey, just as the Lord, the God of your fathers, promised you.
>
> Hear, O Israel: The Lord our God, the Lord is one. Love the Lord your God with all your heart and with all your soul and with all your strength. These commandments that I give you today are to be upon your hearts. Impress them on your children. Talk about them when you sit at home and when you walk along the road, when you lie down and when you get up. Tie them as symbols on your hands and bind them on your foreheads. Write them on the doorframes of your houses and on your gates (Deuteronomy 6:1-9).

The writer (Moses) told them up front that they weren't only supposed to observe the law but also pass it on to their children and their grandchildren. In verse 7 he put some feet to that, telling them exactly how to do it—talking with them morning, noon, and night, and living it out in their actions (hands) as well as in their thinking (their foreheads). The message was clear. Teach your kids values 24-7-365.

Do you wonder how well those parents listened to Moses?

Wanna flip ahead and see?

Let's fast-forward through the book of Joshua, where Joshua took over Moses' job of leading God's people. Then turn to the beginning of the book of Judges. After Joshua died . . . something awful happened:

> Joshua son of Nun, the servant of the Lord, died at the age of a hundred and ten. And they buried him in the land of his inheritance, at Timnath Heres in the hill country of Ephraim, north of Mount Gaash.
>
> After that whole generation had been gathered to their fathers, another generation grew up, who knew neither the Lord nor what he had done for Israel. Then the Israelites did evil in the eyes of the Lord and served the Baals. They forsook the Lord, the God of their fathers, who had brought them out of Egypt. They followed and worshiped various gods of the peoples around them. They provoked the Lord to anger (Judges 2:8-12).

After Joshua and the generation of parents all died, their kids grew up. And according to this passage, these kids didn't know God or what he had done for them. So, lacking any values, they made bad choices and did evil things. This is a sad picture of what happens when parents don't teach their kids values, specifically God-centered values.

AS PARENTS WE NEED TO GRAB EVERY OPPORTUNITY TO TEACH OUR KIDS. DEUTERONOMY 6 SPELLS IT OUT: MORNING, NOON, AND NIGHT.

That's going to mean some radical change for some parents. Many of us are used to bringing kids to church on Sunday for a quick "fill" of Jesus. Sort of like: "Fill 'er up!"

If we're lucky, our kids actually listen to the thirty-minute message in "big church," and then hear the youth pastor give a twenty-minute talk in youth group.

Hey, that's almost an hour! Not bad . . . out of 168 hours per week!

Moses' directives about talking to our kids morning, noon, and night paint a much different picture.

Let's try something else on for size. Let's jump to the New Testament. At the end of the Gospel of Matthew, just before Jesus ascended to Heaven, he gave his disciples a few last words. Historically, this passage of Scripture has been called the Great Commission. Jesus says:

> "Therefore go and make disciples of all nations, baptizing them in the name of the Father and of the Son and of the Holy Spirit, and teaching them to obey everything I have commanded you. And surely I am with you always, to the very end of the age" (Matthew 28:19, 20).

Pretty famous passage: "Go and make disciples."

My friend Greg Stier has taught on this passage and likes to remark that this word "go" would be best interpreted "as you are going." Reread the verses with that understanding: "*As you are going,* make disciples . . ."

As you are going through your day, disciple others. In other words, teach them *how* to actually live for Jesus.

Matthew tells us to do this to *all nations.* Do we think all nations includes our own kids? An alternative would be that he means for us to go disciple some guy from Montana, but ignore our own children. Uh . . . probably not.

MAKING DISCIPLES "AS YOU ARE GOING"

- As we get up in the morning, we should pray with our kids, asking God to give us an eternal perspective throughout the day, even though we live in a world that magnifies the temporary perspective.
- As we are driving them to school and the subject of cheating comes up, dialogue about what's right.
- As we pick them up from school and pass a crowd of mean kids, take a moment and pray for those kids and our attitudes toward people that make us mad.
- As we finish dinner, take a moment and read some Scripture and ask everyone to share one thing they heard.
- As we watch one of our favorite TV shows and something happens that is contrary to biblical teaching, hit the pause button and ask the kids, "What just happened there?" Ask them, "Is that the right thing to do in that situation?" Follow it up with, "How do you know?"
- As we put them to bed, ask them to share one high and one low of their day. Listen to them as they share their heart. Pray for the "low" that they shared.

So this means, *as we are going*, teach our kids how to actually live for Jesus.

Put this together with the Deuteronomy passage and it means something like this: *As we are going, talk with our kids morning, noon, and night, walking along the road and sitting on our couches, teaching them how to actually live for Jesus in day-to-day situations.*

Look for opportunities to make disciples of your kids, building values as you are going.

Making disciples and building values into our kids and teenagers sounds great, but how should we do it? I want to raise godly kids who reflect lasting values, but what does that look like in practical terms? As we are going through daily life, how can we teach our kids lasting values?

TEACHING LASTING VALUES IN DAILY LIFE

I'm sure these aren't the only ones you can use, but here are five principles that have helped me:

1. Set up guidelines
2. Don't overreact
3. Use media to springboard discussions on values
4. Don't be afraid to say no
5. Get them to God's Word for answers

Let's take a deeper look at each of these.

Set up guidelines

We've already heard some research that urged us to raise the bar with our kids and teenagers. Parents who talk to their kids about the dangers of drugs and alcohol help them avoid the consequences of going down that road. This is true in other areas as well.

The American Academy of Pediatrics in 2010 released a study, "Sexuality, Contraception, and the Media." This report examines media messages teenagers are absorbing and how those influences affect their well-being. In other words, when my daughters watch the newest sitcom on ABC, does it make them want to "hook up" with their boyfriend? That's what the AAP sought to discover.

Here are some of the findings that jumped out at me:

- More than 75 percent of prime-time programs contain sexual content.
- Only 14 percent of these incidents mention any risks or responsibilities of sexual activity.
- Talk about sex on TV can occur as often as eight to ten times per hour.
- Between 1997 and 2001 alone, the amount of sexual content on TV nearly doubled.
- The media may function as a "superpeer" in convincing adolescents that sexual activity is normal young-teenager behavior.
- Listening to sexually degrading lyrics is associated with earlier sexual intercourse.
- Of nine studies seeking to determine if "sexy" media contributes to early sexual activity, seven of these studies have shown that exposure to sexual content on TV and other media in early adolescence can as much as double the risk of early sexual intercourse.
- Early exposure to sexual content doubles the risk of teen pregnancy.
- Bedroom TVs are associated with greater substance use and sexual activity by teenagers.

The AAP summarized its findings this way: *"Clearly, the media plays a major role in determining whether certain teenagers become sexually active earlier rather than later."* Let me put it plainly: most teenagers are absorbing way too much sexual content in media, and it's affecting them big time! The consequences are evident. The U.S. Centers for Disease Control and Prevention in 2008 found that more than 3 million teenaged girls—one in every four—had contracted a sexually transmitted disease.[22]

But there's some good news from the AAP report as well:

- Teenagers whose parents control their TV viewing habits are less sexually experienced.
- Adolescents whose parents limit their TV viewing are less likely to engage in early sex.

The report words it like this: "Pediatricians should counsel parents to recognize the importance of the media, exert control over their children's media choices, keep their children's bedrooms free of TVs and Internet connections, and avoid letting their children see PG-13 and R-rated movies that are inappropriate for them."[23]

Those are pretty clear guidelines. In the year prior the AAP encouraged parents to adhere to the following media recommendations:

- Prohibit media in bedrooms.
- Make thoughtful media choices and co-view with kids.
- Limit screen time to one to two hours a day.
- Provide no "screen media" at all for infants and toddlers under two years old.[24]

If you read the Kaiser report cited earlier in this book—the one revealing our kids average more than ten hours of entertainment media daily—you'll read similar recommendations.

I'm amazed at the number of parents who don't set media guidelines when all the wisdom available to us—from the American Academy of Pediatrics to the book of Proverbs—recommends it. Guidelines protect our kids and teenagers.

But I guess some people see such rules as threatening or constricting.

Do you like basketball? Imagine sitting in an arena with tens of thousands of other fans watching an NBA game. A player brings the ball downcourt, faces a little pressure from the guard . . . so he shoves the defender, which is a blatant offensive foul—charging.

But for some reason, the referee doesn't call it. So when the other team has the ball, it decides to test these new waters—an elbow to the rib cage of the defending center. The center is out with a broken rib.

No call once again.

Things are getting heated. The next time the ball is brought down the court, the defensive player hauls off and hits his opponent in the jaw, then grabs the ball. He only gets five steps before he's tackled by another player. The ball drops to the ground and the two players start brawling. Another player turns to his nearest opponent and drills him in the nose. Within seconds, the basketball game has become . . . a hockey game.

The benches empty and before we know it, twenty-plus athletes are on the court beating the life out of one another.

One of the players goes to his car, grabs a bat, and brings it to the court. He begins swinging at any player wearing a rival jersey. Players grab chairs from the sidelines and try to defend themselves. Blood and teeth are flying.

A knife is pulled . . .

OK, this is obviously preposterous. But let me ask you just one question. How stupid are rules like that very first missed call—the one for charging?

WHEN IT COMES TO BASKETBALL, MOST PLAYERS ACTUALLY LIKE THE RULES, THE VERY GUIDELINES THAT KEEP BASKETBALL FROM BECOMING A UFC CAGE FIGHT—OR AN ALL-OUT WAR! RULES HELP US AND PROTECT US.

Don't think that you're doing your kids a favor by lowering the bar. In fact, you're hurting them. Make some guidelines. You can use guidelines like the experts I've cited in this chapter recommend, or you can create your own.

I have some media guidelines in my house. Some of these are adapted from studies like the ones above. Others are from other parenting seminars I've attended and blogs I've read from friends like

Jim Burns, Wayne Rice, Al Menconi, and others. Check them out in the box below.

> **MCKEE MEDIA GUIDELINES**
> - Must tell Mom and Dad what songs you're downloading.
> - We (parents) get all passwords for Facebook, e-mail, etc.
> - We (Mom and Dad) can look at your Internet history, iPod, or cell phone texts at any time.
> - No cell phone use after bedtime. It's turned off—not placed on silent.
> - No TV or Internet in kids' bedrooms.
> - No secular music for the first hour in the morning and the last hour at night.

The last guideline in the sidebar is one I got from Al Menconi. When I first heard it, I honestly thought, *That's silly.* But then our family tried it. There's something about listening to Christian music, especially worship music, first in the morning and then before bed. It sets your mind in the right perspective for the "bookends" of your day. Thanks to a handful of good musicians, I really have grown to like that rule. (Thanks David Crowder Band!)

In case you're wondering, we do allow secular music in our house as long as it doesn't contradict biblical values. I'll talk a little bit more about discernment with music in the next chapter. (It's such a huge issue with teenagers today that I think it warrants the attention of an entire chapter.)

The point is, make guidelines and set up accountabilities that help your kids. In addition to rules regarding the use of media, we have some other guidelines as well, including:

- Curfews—so they get good sleep
- Rewards for good grades
- Software on the computer that keeps them from wandering into trouble online
- Rules about dating and being with the opposite sex

This doesn't mean that your house should become a military school. In my house we have rules that protect our kids, not stifle them from growing up. These guidelines become a little more lenient as our kids get older. I'll go into more detail about this in the next chapter and in chapter 9.

Don't overreact

Whenever I teach a parenting workshop I spend the first hour educating parents about today's youth culture. I show clips from the most popular TV shows, music videos, and movies. I play songs and cite lyrics. I reveal what iTunes, YouTube, and other popular Internet locations provide. I don't show anything pornographic or R-rated . . . and that's the shocking part. I just show the stuff that comes with normal cable or videos that are a click away on iTunes.

Parents are always amazed at how profane the media has become. I usually only show a thirty-second clip of an MTV reality show, typically a montage of hookups, bed scenes, and some half-naked girl (MTV simply blurs the nudity) cursing and fighting with another girl. Parents' jaws hit the ground when they see these videos.

As I finish my presentation, I can almost see steam coming out of the ears of some parents. I know that if I released them at that very moment, they would go home, rip the cable box out of the wall, smash the computer with a baseball bat, and bust their kids' cell phones in half. Parents tend to respond in anger. (If you read chapter 1, you know that I can relate.)

That's why I always tell parents: "Please, take a deep breath and think for a moment. The worst thing you can do right now is overreact. I want you to wait a week and just pray."

PARENTS LOOK AT ME LIKE I'M CRAZY.

But think about everything we've discussed in this book so far. Most of us know how difficult it often can be to open up the avenues of conversation with our kids, especially teenagers, right? Let me ask you, when you read about building relationships with your kid(s) in chapters 3 and 4 . . . did you have the feeling, *I have that mastered*? Do your kids and teenagers open up to you right now and share their hearts? Do they listen to your advice and sit captivated by your every word?

Chances are, it will take a lot of work to build trust with your kids, opening doors to healthy dialogue. And do you know the best way to destroy all that work?

Overreaction.

If you want your kids to close their mouths and their hearts, go home and destroy some technology in a tirade.

Parents need to respond reasonably. A great way to do that is to commit to wait and pray for a certain amount of time. I recommend a week. During this time, collect your thoughts and think strategically about how you'll talk with your kids.

In Acts 17, Paul went to the city of Athens and began looking around, getting a grasp of the Athenian culture. He witnessed idol worship (v. 16) and listened to the pagan poets (v. 28). Verse 16 says that he was "greatly distressed" when he saw all of the idols around the city. As parents, we should be greatly distressed when we see what our kids and teenagers are saturating themselves with daily.

But that doesn't give us license to overreact.

Look at verse 17 and see Paul's response. Paul "reasoned" with the people "day by day," engaging in conversations about their culture, even citing some of their culture to provoke discussion.

We need to follow Paul's example and not overreact.

In my years as a father, some of the best conversations I've had with my kids were on the days following a discovery—when I discovered something they had been doing. I held the reins in all those conversations because they knew they were busted. So when I used those opportunities to listen and reason with them, they welcomed the opportunity (because "reasoning" beats "screaming" any day!).

As you see distressing elements in our culture, use them as opportunities to reason with your kids.

Use media to springboard discussions on values

Many of the media studies I've quoted in this book use this term: *co-watch*. They advise parents to "co-watch" media with their kids. This simply means that, if your kids want to watch a show that you've never seen, you make time to sit down and watch it with them.

Two things can happen:

> 1. You'll watch it for a while and realize, *This is fine*.
> 2. You'll watch it for a while and realize, *This is far from appropriate*.

If it's the first situation, then, worst-case, you've got some time hanging with your kids doing something *they* wanted to do. If the show is more like number two (pun intended), then use it as an opportunity to dialogue with your kid or teenager about the media. The same can be done with songs. (Again, the next chapter has much more on this topic.)

The apostle Paul did this very thing in Acts 17. He actually quoted some of the pagan poets of the day. That's like us quoting lyrics today and using them to "reason" with our kids.

One of the best tools I use to engage in conversation with my kids is the pause button. When we "co-watch" shows as a family, if something pops on the screen that is contrary to biblical teaching, I just hit pause. (Side note: we never watch live TV. God bless DVRs!)

Here's what usually happens. We're watching a cop show or detective show (we like those) and one of the characters makes an offhand comment about "hooking up" or having sex. Usually, I hit pause and ask a question. I might ask blatantly direct questions like, "So, is hooking up something worth trying?" My kids will say, "No, Dad!"

I'll play the devil's advocate (literally). "But why? I mean, this guy's making it sound like it's the thing to do!"

I do this a lot in my house.

Don't get me wrong. Honestly, my kids don't love it. Usually, when I hit pause, my kids all groan, "Dad! We get it! It's bad! Can we just watch the show?!!"

But I persist. Because they know that if a show just makes little comments here and there, I'll use the pause button. If a show digresses to the level of profane or gratuitous garbage . . . then I'll use another button—the "off" button. Which leads me to the next principle about teaching values . . .

Don't be afraid to say no

It's OK to say, "We don't allow this in our house."

A few years ago our family began watching the show *Smallville*. Now I don't want to be a whiner or complainer, and I don't want to give the show a scarlet letter; I just want to share with you our experience.

Smallville is the story of Clark Kent (as in Superman fame) as a teenager. We began watching it as a family and loved it. Season one was a lot of fun. Hey, it's Superman! Good family fun, right?

Well, once or twice the first season I remember thinking, *Whoa! They didn't need to show that.* But it was a pretty innocent show overall.

Then season two came along. Lana Lang began to get a little more trampy as the show went on. Before long we were seeing her and some other girls in revealing attire or even their underwear.

By season three, the show had spiraled downhill. At one particular moment during one of the episodes, I told the kids, "This is getting to be a little too much. If this keeps up, we have to dump this show." We all hated the thought of it because we really had grown to like some of the characters.

The show didn't last another episode before digressing again. My son said, "All right, that's enough." I can tell you honestly, I was proud of him.

It was a sad moment in the McKee household. *Smallville* had a storyline and characters we all enjoyed. But once it began going against biblical values, we dumped it!

You're going to find plenty of media that violates the guidelines you set up. Don't be afraid to say, "Sorry. That doesn't belong in this house."

When I was twelve, I had a friend named Denny (not his real name) on my soccer team. Denny was not a good influence in my life at all. My dad started to notice some of the changes in my language as well as some frequent back talking. He knew I spent a lot of time with Denny, but he really didn't know Denny that well.

One day at a game, Denny yelled at our coach in front of everyone, screaming and cussing. All the parents were quiet. I knew my dad was there. I didn't even look over at him. Twenty minutes later, Denny yelled at his own dad just the same. This was typical Denny. He disrespected teachers and adults all the time. But this time I knew my dad was here to see the whole thing.

SURROUNDING YOURSELF WITH ENCOURAGEMENT

Make sure you nurture relationships with families who hold to the same values as yours. Notice I didn't say "same guidelines." Guidelines will differ, and that's OK. But don't ever give up surrounding yourself with people who encourage you to keep your values (Hebrews 10:25).

Various families respond to media in different ways. I have some good friends who allow their kids to listen to some songs that we don't allow in our house. And we let our kids watch some shows that they don't allow. We both go to the same church, have a faith in Jesus, and hold very similar beliefs on most issues. But our media perception is different. Personally, I see a lot more danger from music than movies, mostly because the average teenager fills his head with music for several hours more per day than he does movies. Our good friends know my opinion about music, and I know theirs about movies. We respect those guidelines. Frankly, I think we've rubbed off on each other in good ways, something like "iron sharpen[ing] iron" (Proverbs 27:17).

Lori and I are involved in a group at church made up of a bunch of parents of teenagers like these—in fact, this group is where we met most of our close friends today. This group is a fantastic place to encourage each other in our relationship with God and help each other in our role as parents trying to raise our kids right.

The game ended and my dad was dead quiet on the way to the car. I could tell he was thinking something over . . . and it wasn't going to be something I liked.

When we got into the car, he shut the door, turned around, looked me in the eyes, and said, "You're never hanging out with Denny again!"

I was livid! Denny had become one of my best friends. And that's part of the reason I was becoming such a little punk! But I was also smart enough not to argue with my dad about it. Besides, secretly I knew he was right.

I LOOK BACK ON THAT MOMENT AND REALIZE THAT MY DAD DID A WISE THING THAT DAY.

Our kids' friends have a huge influence on them. We need to teach our kids Christlike compassion for all people. But they also need to be very careful concerning who they choose to allow in their inner circle of influence. They need friends who will encourage them in their faith (Hebrews 10:25), are devoted toward Christian fellowship (Acts 2:42), and are ready to help them if they stumble (Ecclesiastes 4:9-12). As parents, it's OK to say, "Sorry, you need to pick a new best friend."

Don't be afraid to say no or "this doesn't belong in our house." But be ready to back these guidelines up with solid biblical reasoning.

Get them to God's Word for answers

As you discuss godly values with your kids, always point to God's Word. A big part of building lasting values is being connected to the source those values come from.

Since my wife and I are far from perfect, if their values were based on our example . . . our kids would be messed up. I'm not saying that our example isn't important. It is. As believers in Christ, our foundation is something much greater than even family. A family can fail us, but God will always be there for us.

The Bible is God's Word to us. God has given us such great wisdom in it. My kids have grown up knowing its authority. And it's a guidebook we can use to help teach and correct our children. The apostle Paul said in 2 Timothy 3:16, "All Scripture is God-breathed and is useful for teaching, rebuking, correcting and training in righteousness."

I've heard that verse used incorrectly when people have tried to say that it's a Christian's job to judge the sinner. They don't realize that this verse is actually addressed to believers, and calls us to help correct ourselves before worrying about outsiders. A perfect application of this verse would be authentic parents using Scriptures to correct *themselves* and *their families* in love, humility, and grace.

So how can we use Scripture as a tool to teach values?

Previously I've mentioned how important a time of family Bible reading can be. But don't limit it to those scheduled times. Remember to point to Scripture "as you are going."

Parents will also need to know Scriptures to support their media guidelines. Maybe your family is watching TV together and the show you are watching preaches that recreational sex is not only fun but also commendable! What do you do? Dive into some Scripture to find the truth on the matter. (And there are many!)

Christians often quote Philippians 4:8 as a catchall verse about what's "good" and what's "bad": "Finally, brothers, whatever is true, whatever is noble, whatever is right, whatever is pure, whatever is lovely, whatever is admirable—if anything is excellent or praiseworthy—think about such things."

You can't argue with the beauty and truth in that verse. But I don't know if it's the best one when it comes to backing up our decisions concerning digesting certain media. Yes, it's good to think about praiseworthy things . . . but does watching a TV show actually keep you from thinking about praiseworthy things? It can, depending on the show. But let's look at the whole of the Scriptures—not just one passage—to communicate truth.

I believe Colossians 3:1-10 goes a step further than Philippians 4:8, encouraging us to set our minds on things above, not earthly things. It even provides a list of stuff we should "rid ourselves of" and a description of what our "new self" looks like when we allow Christ to take control of our lives.

The more you dive into God's Word as a family, the more you'll find passages that shed light on day-to-day decision making.

Recently our family finished reading the book of 1 John together in our reading time after dinner. After its reminders about what God's love looks like in us, along with its call to obedience, 1 John ends with this verse: "Dear children, keep yourselves from idols" (5:21). I love the way the New Living Translation renders this verse: "Dear children, keep away from anything that might take God's place in your hearts."

Powerful, eh?

I'm not claiming that *Smallville*, or any other TV show, will necessarily take God's place in your kids' hearts. But we do need to be careful with the distractions that come into our lives.

TALK TO THEM!

All of the above principles are methods I've used to try to build values into the lives of my kids. Most of these principles seem to help Lori and me regularly engage in conversations with them. And that's the common denominator we've noticed from most of the reports and opinions we've read about kids' exposure to media: *Parents, talk with your kids about influences like this.*

Isn't that exactly what Deuteronomy 6 asks us to do?

In the next chapter, we'll go a step further and look specifically at how to not just talk about media with our kids and teenagers, but actually help them begin to develop discernment to make godly decisions on their own.

• CANDID QUESTIONS FOR REFLECTION •

Some Questions for You, You & Your Spouse, or Your Small Group to Ponder

1. WHAT ARE common ways that you see parents "lower the bar" for their kids? What are some of the consequences that result?

2. WHAT ARE some of the mixed messages your kids or teenagers hear from adults?

3. WHAT ARE some ways in which we allow character to take a back seat to "fulfillment" or "accomplishment?"

4. READ DEUTERONOMY 6:1-9 again. We should talk with our kids about God morning, noon, and night, "as we are going" day-to-day. What are some ways that you do that now?

5. WHAT ARE some specific ways in which you could do that more intentionally?

6. WHAT ARE some guidelines you have in your house right now? Can you think of others that you might consider?

7. WHAT ARE examples of some things that you might need to say no to, or say, "Sorry, that doesn't belong in this house"?

8. READ COLOSSIANS 3:1-10. What would happen in your house if you printed these verses and placed them on top of your TVs and computers? How would that impact your day-to-day decisions regarding appropriate and inappropriate use of media in your home?

6

DAD, CAN I DOWNLOAD THIS SONG?

(APPLYING DISCERNMENT IN DAY-TO-DAY DECISIONS)

"DAD, CAN I DOWNLOAD THIS song?"

That's what my fifteen-year-old asked me, hoping to download the song from the iTunes store onto her iPod. If you're a parent, you may have experienced a situation similar to this, seeing that 76 percent of eight- to eighteen-year-olds now own these mobile music devices.[25]

During lunch that day, Alyssa had heard a current R & B song play over the school's PA system (because that's what our public schools often do). There's little wonder why my daughter heard this song at school. It featured a very popular "guest rapper" and had been at the top of the charts for weeks, peaking at number one. In other words, this tune had some serious air time! I had heard it in the airport the weekend prior.

As I shared in the last chapter, my kids have an agreement with my wife and me that they must review the lyrics before downloading any song. We've been trying to teach them to use discernment in what they listen to because study after study shows that music truly affects actions.

So when Alyssa asked if she could download the song, I offered her the same response I always give: "Did you look at the lyrics?"

She answered honestly, "Yeah, but I couldn't tell if they were bad."

You gotta love this situation! Here's my daughter being a normal teenager who likes the sound of a song. She knows the process in our house and she comes to me genuinely seeking an answer of what's right.

Or . . . just hoping I'd say yes!

HEREIN LIES THE STRUGGLE. IN MOMENTS LIKE THESE, I CAN'T HELP BUT SECOND-GUESS MYSELF.

Alyssa is a great kid. Am I monitoring her too much? Should I back off and let her just download what she wants? After all, my rules seem a little more stringent than many other parents I know—even some of those in my church.

Do you ever wonder what to do in these situations?

SALLY AND SHIRLEY

I've encountered two extremes when it comes to making these kinds of decisions as parents. The first extreme is the parent I'll call Sally SoWhat. Sally doesn't monitor what her kids watch or listen to at all.

Sally ignores research concerning the media's impact on kids. For instance, the 2009 American Academy of Pediatrics report warns that "the effect that popular music has on children's and adolescents' behavior and emotions is of paramount concern." Studies like this AAP music and lyrics report confirm that lyrics have become more explicit in references to sex, drugs, alcohol, tobacco, and violence. Furthermore, the doctors authoring the report provide numerous examples of the correlation between media exposure and negative behaviors. The report focuses particular attention to the effect of music videos. Frequent watching of music videos has been related to:

- an increased risk of developing beliefs in false stereotypes and an increased perceived importance of appearance and weight in adolescent girls
- an increased probability that watchers will engage in violence, a greater acceptance of the use of violence, and a greater acceptance of the use of violence against women
- an increased acceptance of date rape
- permissive sexual behaviors
- more acceptance of premarital sex (specifically with those watching MTV)
- increased risky behaviors
- alcohol use[26]

Secular researchers who study the media consumption of teenagers all agree that "understanding the role of media in young people's lives is essential for those concerned about promoting the healthy development of children and adolescents."[27]

Despite these numerous reports, Sally simply responds, "They're gonna hear it at school anyway." Besides, it takes effort to monitor the kids' media decisions, she reasons.

So Sally lets them watch and listen to anything they want. If you want an idea of what kind of content they are listening to today as you read this, you could easily check out Billboard.com and take a peek at the Hot 100 for the most listened to, most played, and most downloaded songs during any given week. Then do a search for the lyrics of these songs. As I look at that list right now and research the lyrics, seven of the ten top songs on this chart have racy, adult content. And according to the latest entertainment media consumption study quoted earlier in this book, Sally is allowing her kids to feed their minds with music like this for an average of 2 hours, 19 minutes every day.

SALLY SOWHAT PARENTING IS VERY COMMON. I SEE IT ALMOST EVERY DAY.

But I've also met parents who are the polar opposite of Sally. I refer to this kind of parent as Shirley Shoebox. Surprisingly, Shirley doesn't look up any lyrics or research any music at all. To Shirley, it's *all* evil! She has completely banned all secular media from the house and tries to shelter her teenagers from any secular influence. Secular music is all bad in Shirley's mind; she even has her own Christian version of the song "Happy Birthday," not bowing to *any* societal conformities.

The Shirleys of this world think that their kids don't ever hear any of the music because often they are homeschooled or attend private schools. (Note: I am *not* slamming homeschooling or private schools—Lori and I homeschooled our own girls during middle school. I'm just noting that Shirley commonly perceives that this prevents her kids from exposure to racy media.) But the reality is, unless Shirley lives in Pennsylvania Amish country, and quarantines her kids to the property, then they *do* hear the music every time they walk through Walmart or go to a friend's house or stumble on it in some other setting.

And for those Shirleys who actually let their kids on the Internet, those kids often hear the music on iTunes and see videos on YouTube without Shirley knowing. I know this because I regularly speak at Christian camps around the country and talk with Shirley's kids from coast to coast. They know many of the current songs and are familiar with the same artists as Sally's kids are.

I often chat with Shirleys after my parenting workshops. They usually maintain that their kids aren't exposed to that kind of garbage. On numerous occasions I've even had the opportunity to talk with their teenagers in their presence. Nine times out of ten, I ask the teen a question like, "Did you know what the song 'Bedrock' was about the first time you heard it?" The teenager usually answers me honestly, confirming that he or she had been aware of the song. This is, of course, followed by Shirley erupting at her teenager, "Where did you hear that song?!!" The teenager almost always says, "At Haley's house" or "At Jordan's house."

Shirley's kids aren't usually taught to use biblical values to make good choices on their own. Instead, the choice is already made for them. *Just cover your ears! It's all bad!*

SO SHIRLEY'S KIDS NEVER LEARN TO DISCERN.

Typically, Shirley's kids can't wait to escape the "shoebox" that she keeps them in, venture out into the real world at age eighteen, and experience everything they've missed while living in the shoebox.

I don't want to be Sally.

I don't want to be Shirley.

THREE MEDIA QUESTIONS

My ministry's Web site (www. TheSource4Parents.com) features a Movie Reviews & Quick Q's page. Each of these movie reviews not only provides our two cents on the film, but it also gives parents three questions they can ask their teenagers after watching the film together. The questions are always the same:

1. What's the message/theme of this movie?
2. How do you suppose we—as serious Christ followers—should react to this movie?
3. How can we move from healthy, Bible-based opinions about this movie to actually living out those opinions?

We also provide answers to these questions to help parents dialogue with their kids and teenagers about the movie.

These three questions don't have to be limited to movies. You can use them for TV and music just the same. Use questions like these to dialogue with your kids and help them start thinking biblically about their media decisions.

ANALYZING MEDIA CONTENT

Meanwhile . . . Alyssa is patiently waiting for me to help her decide if the lyrics of this song are good or bad.

Here goes!

Alyssa hands me the lyrics to the song. "Are these bad?" she asks. "I can't tell."

This is a typical question from Christian teenagers: "Is this bad?" I hear this question all the time when I speak to teenagers across the country. After I give a talk on discernment in our media choices, teens inevitably come up to me and ask if a certain musician is bad.

I usually respond the same way. "It doesn't really matter

how good or bad they are, they're in the exact same boat as us. They need Jesus."

My response is usually met with silence and a blank stare as they think about what I said.

THEN I SUGGEST, "I THINK WHAT YOU REALLY MIGHT WANT TO EXAMINE IS THE MEANING OF THEIR CONTENT. ARE THEY DISTRACTING YOU FROM YOUR RELATIONSHIP WITH GOD, OR HELPING YOU DRAW CLOSER TO HIM?"

That usually starts a pretty interesting discussion. It's always, uh, somewhat fun hearing a teenager try to explain why they think Eminem is helping them with their "effin" relationship with God.

We need to teach our teenagers to think biblically about the media they encounter. They need to think about what distracts them from their relationships with God and what helps them draw closer to God. Our kids don't need a list: *Gaga . . . bad, Lil Wayne . . . bad, Toby Mac . . . good.*

Consider that logic for a moment.

Madonna—good or bad?

OK, now what about Amy Grant—good or bad?

Easy, right? The kosher Christian response is that Madonna is, of course, bad, and Amy Grant is good. Duh!

Oops. Hold on a sec! Amy Grant got a . . . divorce! Now is Amy Grant bad, too?

Where do we get off making those judgments?

Yesterday, when I was talking on the phone with my buddy, I gossiped about somebody. (Honestly, I did, just yesterday. I badmouthed somebody that irritated the both of us, and we had a good laugh about it.)

As soon as I hung up, I knew what I'd done. I'd gossiped. Slandered. The Bible has hundreds of references to this kind of activity, always with the command, "Have nothing to do with . . ." placed in front of it. Yet, I did.

I guess instead of asking whether a song is bad, my daughter should ask my wife, "Mom, is Dad bad?" Lori would have to respond, "Yes. In fact, we all are. We all need Jesus!"

That's just it. We're all bad. (Maybe you should actually stop reading this book right now because the author is bad!)

Or, better yet, perhaps we should stop calling people in the media bad or good and start thinking biblically about our media-usage decisions.

So, when Alyssa handed me the lyrics of the song she wanted to download, I didn't give her a simple "good" or "bad" judgment. Instead, we analyzed the content the best we could.

Here's a snippet of what she handed me, a song called "Down," by Jay Sean, also featuring Lil Wayne. (Any song I use will probably be dated by the time this book comes out, but the principles for teaching discernment remain the same.) Just a portion of the lyrics state:

"PUT ON A SHOW . . . LOSE CONTROL"

Aside from the lyrics themselves (again, I encourage you to do a simple Internet search and pull them up yourself), one of the first things I noticed was that this song also featured the "artist" Lil Wayne. This made me flinch. Lil Wayne is *anything* but a role model. His lyrics are always filthy and degrading to women. His content is almost always about the temporary thrill, not what's best for anyone in the long run.

This song that Alyssa handed me was one of those songs that often might be considered "clean" by many. After all, no cuss words. No obvious descriptions of lewd sexual acts. (Not bad for a song featuring Lil Wayne.)

BUT IT'S NOT ALWAYS EASY TO TELL WHAT A SONG IS JUST BY READING OR LISTENING TO ITS LYRICS. BELIEVE IT OR NOT, SOME ARTISTS TRY TO SNEAK HIDDEN MEANINGS INTO SONGS.

So, one of the things I do is refer to the song's music video. Often, they're available for free viewing on sites like YouTube or Vevo. The music video for this particular song, "Down," provides some enlightening insights into the song's meaning. (This isn't always the case, but today's young people often watch the videos of their favorite songs anyway.) I asked Alyssa if she had seen the video. She responded, "Yeah, a bunch of times at Nikki's house."

So I pulled up the video to take a peek for myself. To be fair, I'm happy to say that this video breaks rank with most of the hip-hop videos that feature hundreds of scantily clad girls writhing sexually while the singer calls them all kinds of foul names. However, it does retain enough elements of this genre of music to cause me concern.

For example, there's the presence of Lil Wayne. I make no apologies for my stance on his art: it's tasteless. Then there's the fact that Sean promises a girl "you are my only," yet he seems to enjoy dancing with several other ladies. Again, it's not the filth that frequently accompanies hip-hop music, but is it the type of content you want your teenager listening to again and again?

When teenagers download music, it's much different than a movie. Teenagers typically only watch a movie once or twice (with some exceptions—kids have been known to obsess over certain films and this isn't healthy either). But teens will listen to songs on their iPods sometimes hundreds of times. Think carefully about what kind of content you want your kids playing over, and over, and over . . .

So I decided to look at the big picture for a moment. I was honest and real with Alyssa.

"So what we have here is a song that seems to be from a guy who wants to 'get down' with a girl—whatever that might mean. Maybe the writer of the song is keeping that vague for a reason. The only hints we have to what that means are in the lines, 'I wanna see how you lose control' and 'Come on and bring your body next to me.' I don't think this guy just wants to play 'Duck Duck Goose.'"

We talked a little bit about the Lil' Wayne lyrics and what those meant. But then I ventured a little further in my reasoning to Alyssa. "Sex is a great thing," I told her candidly. "I really hope that you enjoy sex with your husband some day. You two probably will even listen to romantic music together or read poetry together. Heck, Song of Solomon is pretty graphic, and that's in the Bible. The author is pretty excited about God's creation. Some day you're going to experience that sexual joy . . . and it's good stuff.

"But the question you have to ask yourself right now is, 'Do I, a fifteen-year-old girl, need to be constantly replaying a song in my head about this subject matter? Do I need to be continually thinking about losing control sexually?'"

TURNING TO SCRIPTURE

Since this was my fifteen-year-old daughter, rather than talking about the sexual temptation (not that sex isn't a temptation for young girls), I focused on the area of self-control.

A great passage about self-control is the fruit of the Spirit passage in Galatians 5:22, 23. These qualities, one being self-control, are the results—or fruit—of the Spirit of God at work in us. This passage talks about the battle of two natures: the Spirit of God and the sinful nature. It's a great passage to look at together, because then you can ask your teenager, "Since we know that these two natures are battling each other, do you think we should feed the sinful nature?"

If I was having this conversation with a teenage boy, the self-control conversation would be a good one, but it would also be good to talk about the aspect of losing control sexually.

I might start with this passage:

FLEE FROM SEXUAL IMMORALITY. ALL OTHER SINS A MAN COMMITS ARE OUTSIDE HIS BODY, BUT HE WHO SINS SEXUALLY SINS AGAINST HIS OWN BODY (1 CORINTHIANS 6:18).

I've referred to this verse in many conversations with young men about the lyrics they're filling their heads with or the images they're putting in their minds with music videos, racy TV shows, or movies. (This next little section, particularly, is good for dads to think about for conversation possibilities with your teen sons.) I simply ask, "When you're listening to that song about oral sex, or watching those gorgeous women shake their merchandise, are you thinking about pizza and hot wings?" That always gets a laugh. I laugh with them and say, "Yeah, I don't think so. If you do . . . something's wrong with you. Because any *man* would be thinking about sex." Rarely do they argue with that logic.

At this point I might even jump to Matthew and read Jesus' words about lust.

"YOU HAVE HEARD THAT IT WAS SAID, 'DO NOT COMMIT ADULTERY.' BUT I TELL YOU THAT ANYONE WHO LOOKS AT A WOMAN LUSTFULLY HAS ALREADY COMMITTED ADULTERY WITH HER IN HIS HEART" (MATTHEW 5:27, 28).

Most guys have no problem understanding the concept of lust. We know exactly what lust is. *We do it too often.* (You do remember that this book is titled *Candid Confessions of an Imperfect Parent*, right?) This passage just enlightens us to the truth that it hurts us. This can lead to great discussions about porn and how it can devastate marriages. Bottom line: lust isn't a good thing—at all. And God doesn't want us to do it.

I go on. "In 1 Corinthians 6:18, Paul writes that we should 'flee sexual immorality.'" I ask, "What does *flee* mean?"

Most teenagers give an answer like, "Run away from."

I agree with them. Then I ask, "Do you think listening to music or looking at images that make us think about sex—maybe even lust after women—is *fleeing?*"

AS YOU CAN SEE, THERE ARE MANY DIFFERENT APPROACHES WE CAN TAKE TO TALK ABOUT THE TRUTH OF THE SITUATION. THE POINT IS TO SHINE SOME LIGHT ON THE SITUATION WITH THE TRUTH OF GOD'S WORD.

SCRIPTURE PASSAGES THAT RELATE TO MEDIA DISCERNMENT (AND THE BIG IDEAS EACH IS SEEKING TO GET ACROSS)

- Matthew 5:27-30—anyone who looks at a woman lustfully has already committed adultery; if your right eye causes you to sin, gouge it out
- 1 Corinthians 6:18-20—flee sexual immorality; your body is the temple of the Holy Spirit; honor God with your body
- Galatians 5:16-21—do not gratify the desires of the sinful nature: sexual immorality, impurity, hatred, discord, jealousy . . .
- Ephesians 5:1-12—be imitators of God; among you there should not even be a hint of sexual immorality; let no one deceive you with empty words; find out what pleases the Lord; have nothing to do with the fruitless deeds of darkness
- Colossians 3:1-14—set your hearts on things above; put to death sexual immorality, impurity, lust . . .
- 1 Peter 1:13-16—be self-controlled; don't conform to evil desires; be holy in all you do
- 1 Peter 2:11, 12—abstain from sinful desires; live good lives among pagans so they will see your good deeds

PUTTING IT ALL TOGETHER

When I talked with Alyssa, I added a little icing to the cake. I quoted some research. I'm always researching youth culture—it's part of my job. But most parents can also stay familiar with relevant youth culture research by frequenting parenting Web sites or by subscribing to parenting newsletters and blogs.

I pulled up my blog and told her about some research I had done: "A few years ago, a medical publication called *Pediatrics* did a study and concluded that teenagers whose iPods are full of music with raunchy, sexual lyrics start having sex sooner than those who prefer other songs. The report goes on to say that teens who said they listened to lots of music with degrading sexual messages were almost twice as likely to start having intercourse or other sexual activities within the following two years as were teens who listened to little or no sexually degrading music."[28]

I wrapped up my thoughts. "The Bible is clear about this, and the research is solid. The music does affect you."

Alyssa sighed. "Dang. I really like the song!"

This probably surprised her, but I agreed with her. I told her, "I know. It's really got a good sound, and it's catchy. I kinda like it too. But should we only judge a song by whether we like the sound, or by what we know is right?"

She thought about that for a moment, stirring the carpet fibers with her foot, then looking up at me with her big blue eyes. "By what's right."

Then I did something that was difficult, but necessary, as my kids get older. Something that not all parents should do with their fifteen-year-old, but something I thought Alyssa was ready for. I took a lesson from my buddy Walt Mueller, a youth culture expert. While interviewing him for a podcast, Walt told me that he believes parents have to move from "thinking for their kids" to "helping them think Christianly for themselves." I kicked the decision back to Alyssa. I gave her the power to make the choice.

RELEASING THEM TO DISCERN

I told Alyssa, "Then you know what to do—not what you think sounds cool—but what you think is right. It's your choice."

Some parents seem to be scared to release their teens to this kind of choice. It needs careful thought and prayer for the right timing. We all have to release our kids to start making decisions for themselves at some point in their lives, unless you plan on keeping them in your house until they're collecting social security! So the decision you ultimately have to make is, *When?* When are you going to let them start thinking for themselves?

Parenting is a process that begins with us making decisions for our children when they are young, and eventually arrives at the point where we completely release them to their own decisions when they are out on their own. The time in between should be a segue from being very "hands on" to almost completely "hands off."

I realize not all kids are as easy as Alyssa. If I would have given my thirteen-year-old, Ashley, the choice, being young, she might have said,

"The words don't affect me! I'll go ahead and download it!" Ashley, a middle schooler, needs more guidance from us as to what is acceptable and what isn't. Alyssa, a sophomore in high school, needs less.

Parents often ask me, "Should my son play this video game?" Or, "Should my daughter listen to this song?" Even though I could offer some guidance toward an answer to their question, I hesitate to do this because my response would undo the purpose behind my efforts.

Allow me to explain: The answer to that question is: *Parents must help their kids figure out for themselves if they should listen to this song.* The process itself may be more important than the answer. In other words, if I or some other author or radio personality were to simply say, "No, don't let your kids listen to it," I'd hate to think that parents would default to just answering, "Sorry, Jonathan says no, so that means the song is bad."

Parenting isn't that simple. Parenting is *anything* but simple. The fact is, most teaching opportunities take time, effort, and thought. And if parents are truly living out that Deuteronomy 6:5-7 passage, then we'll be dialoguing constantly with our kids and teenagers about the influences around them, the temptations they face, and the decisions they make. These conversations will require a lot of guidance with younger kids, slowly leading to more freedom as they get older. After all, when they're eighteen, it's really up to them, isn't it?

The difficult task is daily balancing exactly how much guidance our kids need—and when to just back off. The important truth we must realize is that if we neglect to give our kids opportunities to make decisions for themselves and face the consequences for those decisions, then they'll never learn from their failures. Think about this: Do you want your kids' first experiences with natural consequences and failure to be when they are out of the house—or with you at their side?

So I gave Alyssa the choice.

Alyssa decided not to download the song.

Teach your kids values and then give them opportunities to make decisions using those values. That doesn't mean becoming Sally SoWhat. It means equipping them to think biblically about decisions and still allowing them to experience failure in your shadow.

As a parent, I struggle with this balance every day. I'm just confessing . . .

• CANDID QUESTIONS FOR REFLECTION •

Some Questions for You, You & Your Spouse, or Your Small Group to Ponder

1. **TO WHOM** do you relate more, Sally SoWhat or Shirley Shoebox? Why?

2. **WHAT ARE** some of the possible consequences of Sally SoWhat's permissive parenting style? Know of any real-life Sallys? (Don't use their real name if in a group.)

3. **WHAT ARE** some of the possible consequences of Shirley Shoebox's restrictive parenting style? Know of any real-life Shirleys? (Don't use their real name if in a group.)

4. **WHAT RESOURCES** can you use to help you decide if a song's content draws your kids and teenagers toward Christ or away from Christ?

5. **WHAT RESEARCH** or personal stories do you know of that you could share with your teenagers if they wanted to download a song that you deemed as inappropriate?

6. **WHAT SCRIPTURES** quoted in this chapter might help you in this situation?

7. **ARE ANY** of your teenagers ready to start making these discerning choices, in your shadow? If so, what is your battle plan for moving forward in this area?

8. **HOW DO** you think you should respond if your kids make an unwise choice regarding their use of media?

DO IT OR . . .
OR ELSE I'LL . . .

(DISCIPLINE AND FOLLOW-THROUGH)

"WAIT UNTIL YOUR FATHER GETS home!"

I used to hate hearing those words, because those words usually meant that I was in huge trouble and it was time for "the paddle." My dad and I always worked with wood, making furniture, birdhouses—you name it. So my dad always had some pieces of wood molding lying around in the garage—voila, the perfect "paddle."

I don't know how discipline was handled growing up in your home, but in my house, spankings were readily accepted. The only question was, "What tool is best for the job?"

THIS SEEMS ALMOST TABOO TO TALK ABOUT TODAY IN AMERICA. OUR COUNTRY SEEMS TO HAVE LOST THE WILL TO DISCIPLINE OUR CHILDREN. BUT WHEN I GREW UP, SPANKINGS WERE AS COMMON AS ICE CREAM TRUCKS, TREE FORTS, AND KIDS WALKING TO SCHOOL.

My third and fourth grade teachers had big homemade paddles hanging from their walls. Our principal and vice-principal had paddles. It was crystal clear: *you misbehave, you get swats!*

In my home, my mom usually selected a belt as the tool of choice to spank my brother and me. Thom and I didn't mind this, because my mom didn't have much in the way of belt-spanking skills. It's as simple as this—her spankings didn't hurt. I'm not trying to rip on my mom. She's a brilliant woman, a university professor; she's just never been very athletic. This was quite evident, even to us as children, every time she tried to brandish a belt in a somewhat threatening manner.

I remember one particular summer when I was seven and my brother was eight. I don't remember what we did wrong, but I'll never forget the spanking. The verdict was in this particular morning, and we had both been declared guilty. My mom declared, "You know what this means! The belt!"

Thom and I put on our best panic faces—"Oh no! Not the belt!"—while trying hard not to laugh.

Mom went and got a belt out of the closet in the other room while Thom and I quietly gave high fives to each other. As she returned to the room, we both were in character, worried looks on our faces. Thom started pointing to me, "Him first! Him first!" I think his lip even trembled when he said it—truly an Oscar-winning performance!

I feigned the reluctant acceptance of being first and approached my mother. The routine was always the same: She would sit on the ground, we would lie across her lap . . . and then she would try to spank us.

So there I was, lying across my mother's lap, deserving of a spanking, but instead receiving some sort of glute massage. On this particular morning, I was attempting to act like it hurt, but I happened to glance up at my brother, who was biting his lip, trying desperately not to laugh.

He fought the urge.

I fought it.

But soon . . . neither of us could hold back, and we both burst out laughing.

My brother laughed so hard that he fell off the bed. His laughter was now full throttle, which for Thom meant silent and red-faced for four seconds, followed by a huge inhaled snort—which set me into another fit of laughter.

By this time, Mom had pushed me off of her lap, stood up, and walked to the door. And that's when she said it.

"Wait until your father gets home!"

Everything immediately changed.

Laughter turned into begging. "Mom, you don't need to do that! We're sorry. Please, spank us again! I promise, it will hurt!"

Mom wasn't having any of it. We had crossed a threshold. Our case had just bypassed the local courts and was now going to be settled in the supreme court—the paddle!

The remainder of the day consisted of much weeping, pleading, and even schmoozing.

"Mom, look, I drew you a picture. Look how pretty these flowers and green hills look. See the pretty lady in the middle with the halo and the forgiving expression on her face. That's you."

MY MOM WASN'T STUPID. "NICE TRY.
I ALREADY CALLED YOUR DAD. HE'S VERY UPSET."

This was even worse than we first thought. Dad wasn't scheduled to be home for hours. The sheer terror of knowing what was in store for us was dreadful. I could practically feel the sting of the paddle on my butt already.

Have you ever cried for four hours?

Five-thirty PM finally arrived. Thom and I were huddled in my room when we heard the sound of the garage opening. Never has the sound of a VW bug pulling in a garage been so ominous.

My bedroom was right next to the garage, and we could hear every movement through the wall. The bug's mighty engine turned off. A few seconds later, the car door opened, then shut.

Silence.

Thom and I stared at each other, picturing Dad walking over to where he kept his wood moldings leaning against the wall. Just as that picture entered my mind, the sound of boards being shuffled resounded through the wall. *My dad was selecting the perfect paddle!*

Panic set in!

Thom darted into his room.

The front door opened and the entryway floor squeaked and groaned as my dad moved across it. His steps were silenced as they hit the carpeted hallway.

I almost leapt out of my skin when I heard the voice right outside my door.

"Who's first?"

Forget nobility and honor. Thom and I each screamed out the name of the other brother.

In a moment of God's grace, my dad chose my brother first. He walked into Thom's room and shut the door behind him. Through the wall I heard my dad say, "Grab your ankles."

Thom's voice pleaded. "Dad, please. Ground me. I'll do the lawns twice this week. I'll . . ."

My dad's calm voice interrupted. "I said bend over."

My brother started crying. "Please, Dad . . . please . . ."

I think my brother was not complying with my dad's request. Because my dad had to resort to Phase 2: The threat of additional whacks.

"Do you want another swat?" My dad threatened.

My brother's voice changed immediately. "OK, I'm bending over! I'm bending over."

And that's when my dad said the stupidest thing to ever leave his lips. I heard it clearly through the wall. "This is going to hurt me more than it hurts you."

What kind of baloney was this? He didn't even bother to say that one to me anymore, because when he did, I would say, "Well, let's switch places then!"

Through the wall I heard the battle persist. My brother continued to beg.

My dad warned Thom again, "Move your hand."

Thom pleaded. "Dad, please . . ."

"Move your hand, or you'll get another swat."

Then, after a moment of silence, I heard the loud "phwaack!" of the paddle—a sound my brother and I knew all too well—followed by the sound of my brother wailing in pain!

In retrospect, I don't know which was worse, being spanked, or having to listen to the horror of the whole experience just minutes before being spanked myself. (I assure you, my dad never did these swats in anger. This wasn't abuse. My dad was just spanking us the way most people disciplined in those days. Funny . . . there was far less disrespect back then.)

This wasn't an uncommon occurrence in our house: Thom and I would disrespect Mom, Mom would try to spank us, Thom and I continued in our disrespect, Mom told Dad, Dad would spank us . . . and finally, we regretted ever disrespecting Mom.

SPANKING AND BEYOND

The spanking was a good punishment to hold over us. If we began whining about chores or showed signs of disrespect, all my mom had to do was threaten calling Dad. Our behavior would change immediately.

Punishments like spankings are rapidly becoming extinct in this country. Parents that spank are practically deemed as child abusers. Who are the role models of good disciplinarians in this country? It's not surprising that you can't find them. Who are they? Billy Ray Cyrus? Ozzy Osbourne?

I used spanking as a disciplinary measure quite a bit with my kids as they grew up. Spanking wasn't popular among our friends. The most common punishment was the time-out.

When Alec was probably only three or four years old, Lori and I had some friends over and their little girl accompanied them. When she did something wrong, her dad picked her up and said, "It's time for a time-out." He walked across the room with her, sat her in the corner and said, "Now sit there for three minutes." He started his watch and walked away.

Soon the kids were playing together again and Alec got angry, grabbed a toy away from his guest, and yelled "Mine!"

Alec and I had dialogued about the concept of sharing many times. He knew that yelling in anger wasn't appropriate. (Unless coming from Daddy. Yeah, not a great example, I realize. More on this in chapter 9.) So I went over to Alec and asked him, "Alec, do you need a spanking?"

Alec looked up at me, pondered for a moment, and then quickly insisted, "No, I just need a time-out!"

People vary in their parenting methodology, and different situations call for different responses: time-outs, spankings, taking away privileges (such as no phone for a week or confiscation of the car keys). Which is correct? Is discipline really needed? Which of these methods is correct? Does it seem uncaring to punish our kids?

Remember the mom in the grocery store (introductory chapter), yelling at her kid, "Don't touch that cereal box or you've got another thing coming!" . . . only to ignore her child when he grabbed the box again, slobbered on it, and banged it on the cart? Most parents have faced a moment like this, a moment when the kid tests the parent's will to *follow through*. He's thinking, *Mom said it. Does she really mean it?*

When our kids are young, many of us set the stage for how discipline will be handled for the rest of their lives. Some kids quickly learn that when Mom says something, she really doesn't mean it. Other kids learn immediately, "Oh, Mom was serious!"

PROVING THAT YOU CARE

If parents choose to let their kids roam free and live undisciplined lives, they're actually hurting them. The book of Proverbs uses a stronger word than hurt: *hate.*

> **THOSE** WHO SPARE THE ROD OF DISCIPLINE HATE THEIR CHILDREN. THOSE WHO LOVE THEIR CHILDREN CARE ENOUGH TO DISCIPLINE THEM (PROVERBS 13:24, *NLT*).

Pretty strong words from Solomon, one of the best sources of wisdom, as true today as it was when it was written. A few verses earlier, he had begun this section with: "A wise child accepts a parent's discipline" (Proverbs 13:1, *NLT*). Solomon was far from perfect, but, unlike his brothers, he did obey his dad. And in his God-given wisdom he advises us not to lower the bar with our kids. In today's language he'd say something like, "If you refuse to discipline your kid, then you're proving to him that you don't care about him."

In an episode of the powerful television drama, *Friday Night Lights*, a teenage girl named Becky was abandoned by her mom and stepdad. Out on her own, she found her way to the house of one of the young football coaches, Billy, and his new wife, Mindy. The young couple took Becky in, realizing that she had no place to go. Within the first week of staying there Becky stayed out late at a party, coming in in the middle of the night. Billy and Mindy were in the front room waiting for her. Mindy laid into Becky, saying something like, "Do you know how worried we've been?"

Becky was shocked. She finally managed to say, "Sorry. I've never had anyone who cared."

Many teenagers might think, and even verbalize, a desire to be able to do whatever they want—such as staying out as late as they want.

BUT IF THEY REALLY STOPPED TO THINK ABOUT IT, THEY'D
PROBABLY COME TO THE SAME CONCLUSION THAT BECKY DID: THE PARENT
WHO LETS HIS KID DO WHATEVER HE WANTS *DOESN'T CARE.*

Kids who ignore discipline are headed toward a difficult journey. Proverbs makes that clear, too: "Whoever disregards discipline comes to poverty and shame, but whoever heeds correction is honored" (13:18).

I ALWAYS FIND IT INTERESTING TO SEE HOW KIDS WHO
AREN'T USED TO DISCIPLINE ACTUALLY RESPOND TO DISCIPLINE.

A couple years ago, I volunteered as a track coach at my daughter's junior high school. The school only provided two coaches for more than a hundred kids. Overwhelmed, they basically had been ignoring the kids who wanted to run distance races like the 800 or the mile. My daughter wanted to run the mile, but often was stuck running sprints or throwing a shot put, simply because the coaches didn't have enough help to monitor all the different events.

Being a distance runner myself, I told the coach that I was happy to help with the distance kids. He gladly accepted. Next thing I knew, I had about twenty to thirty kids show up each day to run endurance runs. They didn't know much more than the fact that they ran the mile fast in PE class.

The first day of practice was a wake-up call for these kids as I announced the workout. "Today we're running 400 repeats. We only will be running eight of them . . . unless you complain. Then I'll add more."

A 400 is one lap around a track. Four hundred repeats are simply running a lap, resting for about a minute, and then running another. They are grueling, and they build speed and endurance. By the second lap, the complaints started coming.

"Coach. I've got a cramp. Please!"

I ignored the complaints and simply responded, "Hey, Justin wants us all to run another lap. We now have nine 400 repeats! Keep complaining and you'll do more."

Kids didn't like me very much by the end of practice.

My decision to follow through on my promise of "more 400 repeats" was not a very popular one. But, as each of my distance kids came out of the locker room, I spent time talking with them. I said things like, "Madison, you have some amazing speed out there. You're going to be amazing when you build up that endurance. It might not feel like it now, but what you did today is going to make you much faster."

Madison and the others would look at me with a look that said, "Really?" Or maybe even, "Are you insane?"

Then I'd add, "I'll see you tomorrow."

I lost about ten runners that first week. Some kids couldn't handle the discipline. But those who stuck with me accomplished amazing feats. A dozen of the kids made it to sectionals. A handful of them made it to the regional meet. One kid, Jared (not his real name), was an overweight kid—by far the slowest kid on the team. Jared lost more than ten pounds during track season and was cheered on by his teammates as he crossed the finish line each week.

At the end of the season I treated them all to a pizza party, where I gave kids awards based on their effort. At that party, parents cornered me and thanked me for teaching their kids to work hard for something. Every one of them said something like, "Wow, I don't know how you did it, but . . ."

One parent laughed and said, "On the first day of track, Kari came home and told me, 'We've got a new coach, and he's mean!'" We laughed. Then she said, "But after one week, she realized that you truly cared."

Kari had four dads in the last twelve years. Most of them had let her do whatever she wanted. When Kari walked out on my track, she had a rude awakening as to what discipline looked like. But in a week's time, she recognized it as someone who cared about her enough to want her to succeed.

IN THE LAST FIVE YEARS I'VE READ HUNDREDS OF STUDIES ABOUT PARENTING AND DISCIPLINE. THE FINDINGS ARE ALWAYS SIMILAR. PARENTS WHO IGNORE THEIR KIDS AND AREN'T AWARE OF THEIR ACTIVITIES PUT THEIR KIDS AT RISK.

"Those who spare the rod . . . hate their children." It doesn't get any more direct than that.

A study done a few years ago by the National Center on Addiction and Substance Abuse at Columbia University reported that a third of teenagers and *nearly half* of seventeen-year-olds attend house parties where, even though parents are present, teens drink, smoke marijuana, and even use exotic drugs like cocaine or ecstasy. That's a lot of teenagers using drugs and alcohol right under their parents' noses!

Former U.S. Secretary of Health, Joseph A. Califano Jr., chairman of the Center on Addiction and Substance Abuse, said, "Teen drinking and drugging is a parent problem. Too many parents fail to fulfill their responsibility to chaperone their kids' parties. The denial, self-delusion and lack of awareness of these parental palookas put their children at enormous risk of drinking and using illegal and prescription drugs."[29]

It's that simple. If you don't care enough to monitor your kids and set guidelines, you are hurting them.

HOW DO WE DO IT?

Most of us wouldn't argue that our kids need to be disciplined. The bigger question is, *How* should we discipline? How can we determine what punishment is appropriate for a given situation?

When our kids were young, Lori and I read various parenting books as we tried to decipher how to discipline and which were appropriate punishments. Opinions varied. Some experts were big fans of spankings, as long as they weren't done in anger. (Whoops. That ruled out some of the spankings I had given. You remember this book's title, right?) Others thought that spankings were abusive. And it's true: one of the biggest mistakes parents make as disciplinarians is enforcing the rules in anger.

Against popular opinion, we finally decided that we would spank if the situation called for it, but never without a conversation first.

As our kids grew older, I wish we had maintained this policy of discipline. Not spanking, but *always having the conversation first.*

Years ago I was sitting on my couch working on my laptop. Alec came in the room with his head hanging low. He was in seventh grade and progress reports had just come out. He knew that the piece of paper he held in his prepubescent hand was going to be the catalyst for incredible conflict in the house that afternoon. So Alec did what most kids his age do; he began giving excuses of how this teacher was unfair, and how that teacher was mean . . .

If you had been standing outside my house at that moment, you might have heard a rumble, then seen all the windows blow out as a huge bomb went off inside the living room—a bomb known by all in my house as Dad!

My content is good. My delivery, however, has had its struggles.

Two hours later, Alec was crying and Lori was pleading with me: "Jonathan, enough. Let's deal with this later." And the girls, the dogs, the cat, and the neighbors were all hiding, trying to stay out of the blast radius.

Don't fall into the temptation of disciplining in anger. It's short-sighted and it hurts the relationships that you've spent so much time and energy building. Instead of reacting quickly, use a simple, effective tool: delay your response.

A delayed response looks like this:

"I'M NOT HAPPY ABOUT THIS AT ALL. THERE ARE GOING TO BE REPERCUSSIONS. DON'T SAY A WORD TO ME NOW. WE'RE GOING TO TALK ABOUT THIS LATER."

This is a recycled version of "Wait until your father gets home." The beauty of this punishment is threefold. Let's unpack the benefits of each.

A delayed response gives you time to think

I don't know about you, but I need some time to calm down and gather my senses. I have a history of angry outbursts, so the best thing for me is to step away from the situation, pray, and come back with a reasonable response.

I don't know why I would ever *not* do this.

Last fall, my daughter Alyssa did something I thought was a flagrant act of disobedience. I found out about it through a text message—a text message she intended to send someone else, but ended up in the inbox of my phone.

Here's the beauty of the situation. By God's grace, Alyssa and I were walking out the door on the way to breakfast together when I noticed the text. Lyssy and I have breakfast together once a week. It's exactly what I talked about in chapter 4—quantity time together, often resulting in quality time.

God gave me the strength to take a deep breath and *not* overreact when I received the text. Literally, as I was walking to the car with her, I sent a quick prayer up to God and asked him, "Lord, please let me get to the truth of this without blowing up. And help me not to ruin this special time that Lyssy and I get together each week!"

We went to the same greasy diner we always go to and ordered our usual breakfasts. The conversation flowed nicely, and she eventually mentioned something about being a little depressed lately. So I started asking questions, not like a parole officer, but as a caring friend.

She opened up and shared some deep personal feelings. I asked her how she was responding to these feelings. She answered honestly, and I replied using a good counseling tool. "How's that working for you?" I asked.

It was at that moment that she surprised me. She talked about some conversations she was having with Christian friends about her feelings and how those conversations led her to search the Scriptures for counsel. Sure enough, she had looked up some verses and was seeking comfort for these feelings. As she was texting a friend back and forth about this, she sent the text that had ended up in my inbox—and a text that had completely new meaning now that I had heard about it in context.

The whole time she was telling me this, she had no clue I had received the text. I eventually told her about the text and we laughed about it.

An interesting side note to this story: When I dropped her off at school I went home and opened my Facebook account. Alyssa had posted a Scripture verse the night before, about the same time she sent out "the text." I looked through her Facebook and read her posts from the last few days. Everything I had just discovered at breakfast was there in plain sight. This made me realize two things: everything she had told me was true, and how sad it was that it took me this long to discover it.

As an added kick in the pants, my dad called me moments later and asked, "How's Alyssa? Her Facebook posts sound like she's a little depressed." I laughed to myself. *Nice that everyone else in the world knew before I did.*

Our kids are often expressing their feelings for all to see. The question is, are we taking time to notice, and do we know where to look?

Looking back at the situation, I thanked God for giving me the strength to stop and think before overreacting. My first response would have not only been based on false assumptions, it would have closed doors that have taken a long time to open.

As parents, it pays to delay our reaction.

A delayed response is a punishment in itself

Instead of giving a punishment right away, make them wait. Let your kids marinade for a while in the realization of being caught. Not knowing can be much worse than knowing.

I use this a lot with my kids, most often because of reason #1 above—I don't want to explode on them. But I've learned that this waiting period is a punishment in itself. My kids hate waiting for the jury. My son will sometimes beg, "Come on, Dad, just tell me what's going to happen! I hate waiting."

I usually milk it for all it's worth. "Sorry, son. Your mother and I need to figure out what to do."

He hates it. Serves him right for disobeying!

A delayed response gives kids time to ponder

As our kids sit in their room simmering in the juices of their own bad decisions, they'll often think through their actions. Some kids will even replay the event in their mind again and again—maybe because they're trying to think of excuses for their actions or an escape from their punishment. No matter. At least they are thinking through what they did. Some might actually experience regret.

Don't feel guilty about using this methodology. This is a little dose of "Welcome to real life." Think about this in the typical workplace. Employee steps out of line. Boss realizes it. Boss pulls employee aside at 10 AM. "We need to talk. Come to my office at four o'clock." Employee sweats three gallons of perspiration over the next six hours!

Don't be afraid to delay your response. It prevents explosions, it's a punishment in itself, and it forces them to think through their actions.

CONFRONTING IN LOVE

But you can't delay the inevitable forever. Eventually, you have to confront your kids and talk with them about their actions.

How do we do this?

Start by remembering the relationship. We've spent almost a third of this book talking about how to build relationships with our kids, spending time and effort to look for communication arenas and opening the doorways to honest communication. Don't lose all of what you've gained in one moment of confrontation.

Don't get me wrong. I'm not saying, "Don't confront." Confrontation and discipline are necessary. But we need to do these things in a loving way. I recommend three steps.

Step One: Set the stage of love and grace

After our kids have stewed in the punishment of our delayed response long enough, invite them in to talk about the situation. If they've been in their room, invite them out to the couch, to the back patio, to coffee . . . anywhere where they feel comfortable talking with you.

Start by asking them how their day was. You can use the trusty ol' "What was the best thing that happened to you today, and what was the worst?" Chat with them for a while, just like you do in their communication arena. Laugh, if possible. Tell them you love them.

Let them know, not only in words, but by your entire demeanor, that you love them unconditionally. In other words, there is nothing they could do to lose your love for them. Assure them, "Even though our family goes through conflict at times, it doesn't stop us from loving each other."

Once you've communicated your unconditional love, move to step two.

Step Two: Define the problem

Sometimes we parents assume that our kids know what they've done wrong. This is a mistake.

At times I've punished my kids on a whim, they've taken the punishment (possibly in fear of an explosion), and then days later, I asked them, "You know why you got busted the other day, right?" More often than I can remember, my kids have responded, "Not really. I just didn't want to argue."

WHAT GOOD IS THAT?
HOW ARE OUR KIDS GOING TO CORRECT BEHAVIORS IF
THEY DON'T EVEN KNOW WHAT BEHAVIORS THEY NEED TO IMPROVE?

Make sure that they know what they've done and, more importantly, the correct action.

One of the best ways to do this is to put the ball in their court. Give them a chance to verbalize what they've done, maybe even recommend a punishment.

After delaying your response, then sitting down with them and communicating your love, ask them about the situation outright. "Why did you get in trouble?"

I did this with Ashley a few years ago when she was in the middle of fifth grade and got in trouble at school. Ashley has always been the most ornery and mischievous of our three—or, as my wife puts it, "the most like her father!" As I picked her up from school one day, her teacher informed me that she had started a little casino of sorts during recess.

Kids at Ashley's school were awarded "Beaver Bucks" for doing well in class. (Her elementary school mascot was the beaver.) So when kids received good grades on a test—two Beaver Bucks. Help the teacher staple papers—a Beaver Buck. Good behavior—a Beaver Buck. Kids could then spend these Beaver Bucks at the end of the quarter at book fairs, carnivals, and other school events.

During this time, my brother Thom had apparently taught my young troublemaker to play poker. (Thanks, Thom!) Ashley thought it would be good to pass on this knowledge to all her little friends at recess.

Imagine the surprise of the teacher on playground duty when she happened upon a table near the far field. Ashley had a stack of Beaver Bucks in front of her and she was saying, "OK, everyone. Seven card stud, and one-eyed Jacks are wild! Ante up!"

I told Ashley we'd talk about it when we got home.

It was a quiet drive.

When we got home, Ashley started crying as she went up to her room. That was one of the tougher moments—letting her feel that pain for a moment. But after about a half hour I called her downstairs.

Ashley loves it when I make fires, so I threw some logs in the fireplace and asked her, "Wanna light the fire?" She smiled and lit the fire.

We talked for a few minutes. I asked her how school was going, about her favorite subject, and for the latest on Chelsea, her class pet, a chinchilla. All things she liked talking about. Ashley is an exceptional student, so it was pretty easy for me to tell her how proud of her I was and let her know that I loved her no matter how many times she got in trouble.

Then I finally cut to the chase. "Ashley, do you want to tell me about the Beaver Bucks?"

Ashley looked up at me and burst into tears.

I motioned for her to come over to me on the couch and she jumped up into my lap. I let her cry for a while, then I told her, "Tell me what happened."

THIS IS IMPORTANT. LET YOUR KIDS TELL THEIR SIDE OF THE STORY. GIVE THEM A CHANCE TO SHARE ALL THE DETAILS.

If their details conflict with the details you received, then calmly go through the painstaking process of finding out the truth. If you need to call a teacher or another parent to verify details, do so as soon as possible. Then simply tell your kid, "Sorry, this is what Mrs. Bolyard said. Is she lying?"

Usually, you can get to the bottom of the matter. Once you do, keep the ball in their court and ask them why what they did was wrong.

This was interesting with Ashley. She didn't really understand the problem with "just playing cards." (Again, thanks, Uncle Thom!) So I explained to her that playing games isn't a problem, but gambling is a problem, especially when you're winning hard-earned Beaver Bucks off other kids! (And yes, that was very hard to say without laughing!)

Help your kids understand what they did wrong. Have them verbalize it. Then, step three . . .

Step Three: Administer the punishment

This can be one of the most difficult steps. That's why I like to let my kids have first shot at it. I let them suggest an appropriate punishment.

This not only buys you time to think, once again, but it also gives them a chance to think through what they did and what would help them learn their lesson.

Whenever I do this with my kids, they usually come up with something better than I would have. In the case of Ashley and the Beaver Bucks scandal, I think she came up with something like writing letters of apologies to the kids and the teacher. Lori and I loved the idea. *And so it was written, and so it shall be done.*

For the few times when your kid may suggest something pretty weak because they don't want to face the music, I suggest telling them that you've heard them, but think 'X' or 'Y' punishment is more appropriate, and carefully explain why.

Consider how effective this approach is compared to just yelling at your kid in anger. Responding in anger not only closes doors of communication, it robs our kids of the opportunity to learn from the consequences of the situation.

Let's be honest: responding patiently and lovingly is a lot more difficult. It takes more time and energy. It's much easier to just yell at our kids and call them morons!

MOST OF LIFE'S VALUABLE ELEMENTS REQUIRE HARD WORK. AND I CAN THINK OF VERY FEW THINGS MORE VALUABLE THAN MY RELATIONSHIP WITH MY KIDS.

Love them enough to discipline them. Remember: "Those who spare the rod of discipline hate their children."

Replace overreaction with a delayed response. Give yourself time to breathe, as well as time for them to sweat a little and think it over.

Finally, confront in love. Let them know how much you value them through tough times. Help them understand what they did and why it was wrong. Discipline them in a way where they learn not to do it again. If you don't, you'll be hurting them way more in the long run.

• CANDID QUESTIONS FOR REFLECTION •

Some Questions for You, You & Your Spouse, or Your Small Group to Ponder

1. **HOW WAS** discipline implemented in your home when you were a kid? How did that work for you?

2. **HOW DO** you discipline your kids now? How's that working for you?

3. **WHY DO** you think the Bible tells us we *hate* our kids if we don't discipline them?

4. **WHAT'S THE** most difficult part of enforcing discipline in your home now? Why do you think this is hard?

5. **SHARE A** time when you disciplined in anger—and what resulted.

6. **WHAT ARE** some ways that you try to avoid disciplining in anger?

7. **WHAT ARE** some specific ways you make your kids feel loved by you when they do wrong?

8. **WHAT ARE** some ways that you can choose what punishment is appropriate for a certain action?

8

I WANT TO BE LIKE YOU, DAD AND MOM

(IMPERFECT PARENTS INSPIRING BY EXAMPLE REGARDLESS)

IT'S NOT EASY GROWING UP as the pastor's kid in a large church. Everything you do is noted and recorded by thousands. That kind of reputation is hard to live down.

When I was ten our family moved to Sacramento, California, and my dad started a church of a few hundred. Hundreds grew to thousands, and by the time I was a teenager, I had quite a reputation as a troublemaker among "the flock." I don't blame the people for worrying about me. My actions *should* have raised concern, especially from the parents of my friends. I once tied up my friend, put him in the trunk of my car, drove crazily, and got into an accident—all with my friend still bound up in the trunk; I filled up the church's baptistery with milk for a game of bobbing for bananas; I even tried to stack tables and chairs high enough to reach the ceiling in our church gymnasium. (It was, however, an amazing sight.)

Not a week went by that my dad wasn't hearing complaints from someone in the church. Of course, thanks to some of the church's "knitting circles," whenever I did something mischievous, within twenty-four hours the entire church knew.

Twenty years later I returned to the church with my own kids. At first, my kids heard a lot of "Your father was quite a troublemaker." But eventually the whispering and pointing faded.

I've always been completely honest with our kids about my past. I hope that they can learn from some of "Daddy's mistakes." So whenever the kids have asked me questions about my teenage years, I'm completely candid.

Lori always cringes when I tell some of my stories. "Jonathan, how do you expect them not to act this way when you did?"

I always defend myself and argue, "But I'm telling them about the mistakes I made, including the consequences."

Unfortunately, I don't always remember to include the consequences in every story. Sometimes my stories are just fun entertainment. Like the time a group of my friends and I climbed up the metal ladder bolted to the side of our church sanctuary and played hockey on the church roof! I shared that story with my kids when I passed by the ladder one Sunday, quickly to be hushed and given the evil eye by Lori. "Jonathan!"

I acted clueless. "What?"

Last October Lori and I were sitting on our couch together having an evening alone. Ashley was at soccer practice, Alyssa at a Bible Study at church, and Alec at work.

The phone rang.

I answered.

It was the head pastor's wife, Karen. "Um, I don't want you to worry, but I wanted to share an incident that happened with Alyssa tonight." She paused.

Moments like these always occur in slow motion. Seconds feel like hours. My gut clenched. What could have happened? *Kidnapping? Murder? Was she bitten by a rabid chipmunk?*

Karen continued. "Somehow Alyssa got the idea that it would be fun to climb onto the church roof."

I breathed a sigh of relief, while at the same time fearing the repercussions I was about to face from Lori, who had just been proven right! (A huge blow for a husband!)

Karen continued. "Apparently, Alyssa talked her friend Natalie into going up with her. Unfortunately, Natalie is afraid of heights. So Natalie wouldn't come down until several adults fetched the giant maintenance ladder and guided her down. It was quite the endeavor."

I apologized to Karen, as best as possible, while being poked in the ribs by Lori. Karen was nice. She made it clear that she wasn't angry; she just wanted to let me know what had happened.

When I hung up the phone I ate enough crow to last a year.

ACTIONS SPEAK LOUDER . . .

If you want to block inappropriate content on your computer, there are a variety of programs and settings you can use to protect your kids. But I think you'll be hard-pressed to find any "inappropriate content" blockers to protect kids from what they hear from their parents. I know I've needed one attached to my mouth many times.

A few years ago one of my kids played on a team where one of the parents was a loose cannon, to say the least. Her mouth was out of control. If she wasn't busy bad-mouthing another parent or a kid on the team, then she was hollering at the ref with a few expletives inserted into the mix.

The ironic part? She was always the one correcting all the girls on the team for saying words like "crap."

IN NEARLY TWO DECADES OF BEING A PARENT, THERE IS ONE THING I'VE LEARNED CRYSTAL CLEAR: YOU CAN TEACH WHAT YOU KNOW BUT YOU CAN ONLY REPRODUCE WHAT YOU ARE.

When I was a senior in high school, I had the privilege to be a summer camp counselor for a group of fourth through sixth grade students from my church. I became responsible for a dozen fourth grade boys for the week. Being a role model for young boys was a huge task for a teenager.

I discovered something right away. Fourth grade boys didn't listen very well whenever I gave instructions like "brush your teeth" or "clean up the cabin." But when I happened to say something edgy or even slightly inappropriate, they had ears like a fox!

"Jake! Get your stinking butt in the cabin!"

Eleven kids became eleven parrots. "Ha! *Stinking butt!*" "Yeah Jake, get your *stinking butt* in the cabin!!!" "*Your butt stinks!!!*"

Is it just me, or do you find that our kids rarely misquote us? In fact, they usually quote us word for word concerning something that we shouldn't have said in the first place.

During this week as a camp counselor I was able to get just a taste of the overwhelming mentoring responsibility parents have for their kids. For seven days straight, twenty-four hours a day, kids watched me, mimicked me, and quoted me.

One day I decided to take the kids up to the BB gun range. Each of us were given a BB gun by the attendant at the range and given a short lecture on safety—simple, logical rules like:

- never aim the gun at another person
- never go up and check your target while others are still shooting at their targets

Before long all twelve kids and myself were lined up at the range shooting at the targets. As soon as each kid ran out of BBs, he was instructed to wait for the others, and then all would check their targets together.

Did I mention that these were fourth grade boys? Patience isn't a strong suit for that age.

When the first kid emptied his gun, immediately we all heard it. "I'm done! Can I check my target?"

"As soon as everyone else is done," I'd answer matter-of-factly. Another kid would finish. "I'm done. Can I go check my target?" Again: "As soon as everyone is done!"

Two more kids finished. "We're done. Can we check our targets?"

My voice showed a little less patience this time. "AS SOON AS EVERYONE IS DONE!"

A kid named Chris finished at this point. He didn't ask, he just marched toward his target to see how he did . . . despite the fact that seven other boys were still shooting targets, some of them less than two feet from his target.

"Chris! Get back behind the line!" I barked. "You're gonna get shot!"

Chris didn't stop or even slow down. He actually sped up, saying, "Just let me check it really quick."

"*CHRIS!* Get behind the line!" I yelled.

Chris ignored me and ran up to his target.

That's when it happened. I don't really know what I was thinking. I probably *wasn't* thinking; I was just responding to my emotions.

I pulled up my gun and shot Chris in the butt! "Chris, get behind the freaking line!" I shouted.

Chris grabbed his butt and started hollering in pain.

And that's when utter chaos broke loose, something I never would have predicted at the time. Eleven other kids burst out laughing . . . and then simultaneously lifted up their guns and started shooting Chris, again and again. Chris was jumping around like he broke open a bee-hive. It was *horrifying* and, dare I say . . . *hilarious* at the same time.

I immediately began yelling. "Everyone stop!" But they weren't listening. It was *Lord of the Flies* all over again. They were all madly shooting, cocking their guns, and shooting again. Within five seconds, Chris had taken over fifty shots to the body, and two to the face. He eventually dove behind a hay bale.

It took me several minutes to calm the kids down and collect all the weapons. Aside from a bunch of red welts, Chris was fine. But I was banned from the BB gun range for the week and had to go see the camp director.

I LEARNED A VALUABLE LESSON THAT DAY. THERE IS NO TRUTH AT ALL TO THE OLD SAYING, "DO WHAT I SAY, NOT WHAT I DO."

It would be nice if our kids always listened to what we said and obeyed perfectly. In actuality, they are doing much more than listening—they are watching. Like it or not, we are being watched.

On the bright side, this means that they will notice when we respond in compassion to the homeless person who asks us for money, and they'll see us give back the extra $20 that the Walmart clerk incorrectly counted back to us. Sadly, they'll also see us yelling at our spouse, breaking seemingly insignificant traffic laws, or perhaps gossiping about an annoying neighbor.

Regardless of the moral stand we preach, our true values are exposed by our actions. Our kids will copy what we do much more than what we say.

When I was young I heard an old preacher tell a story that I've never forgotten. He told about a time when American settlers began to have peace talks with the Native Americans in the region.

At one particular meeting the settlers were trying to convince these so-called "Indians" to enter into a treaty with them. The wise old Indian chief listened carefully to every word the settlers said. When the settlers were finished, he spoke.

"I've heard everything you, the white man, has said. What the white man says makes sense. If what the white man says is true, then this is a good agreement."

But then the old chief surprised the settlers with his next words. "We have decided that we will wait and watch the white man for a while."

The settlers were confused. "I don't understand. I thought you said that this agreement makes sense and sounds good?"

The chief replied. "What you say makes sense. It does sound like a good agreement. But we find that what the white man *says* and what the white man *does* are two different things. So, we will watch the white man for a while. If what the white man *does* matches what he *says*, then we will make an agreement."

Wise old man.

For thousands of years people have noticed this difference between talk and actions. That's probably why Peter urged early Christians to be careful how they lived their lives around their unbelieving neighbors. Check it out: "Be careful to live properly among your unbelieving neighbors. Then even if they accuse you of doing wrong, they will see your honorable behavior, and they will give honor to God when he judges the world" (1 Peter 2:12, *NLT*).

In the prior verse, Peter warned believers to watch out for "worldly desires." One of the biggest reasons for this is that we are being watched by the world.

THEY ARE TAKING NOTE OF THE WAY WE TALK AND THE WAY WE TREAT OTHERS. OUR CHRISTIAN BUMPER STICKERS AND T-SHIRTS DON'T DEFINE US, OUR ACTIONS DO. THE WORLD IS OBSERVING OUR ATTITUDES.

INSPIRING OUR KIDS

As parents, our audience lives with us. We are in the spotlight 24/7. Our words don't affect our kids half as much as our actions do. We need to inspire by example.

I see at least three ways we can be an inspiration to our kids.

Be honest about your own imperfections

All of us are imperfect—it's undeniable. Don't be afraid to let your kids know that *you* know this. And this brings up the elephant in the room. Do you know your own imperfections? Or are you the only one who may not see the glaring problem that you have? The road to healing begins by admitting you have a problem.

Once you admit it to yourself, admit it to your kids. "Hey, Dad has been messing up."

Sometimes your kids will see you mess up with someone else. Apologize to that person—and apologize to your kids as well.

No one said parenting was easy.

Here's the good news. Our kids don't need an unblemished hero they can't relate to. Our kids need a role model who is real and has wrestled with similar struggles.

Break free from your imperfections

All of us mess up. But what kind of role model are we if we keep returning to the same mistakes? In Hebrews, the author wrote:

THEREFORE, SINCE WE ARE SURROUNDED BY SUCH A GREAT CLOUD OF WITNESSES, LET US THROW OFF EVERYTHING THAT HINDERS AND THE SIN THAT SO EASILY ENTANGLES . . . LET US FIX OUR EYES ON JESUS, THE AUTHOR AND PERFECTER OF OUR FAITH (HEBREWS 12:1, 2).

This passage lays it out: first, throw off the sin that hinders. All of us are probably quite familiar with what that is in our own lives. The question is: How do we throw it off?

Let me dive into a very alluring sin for men: lust. In 1 Corinthians 6:18 Paul instructs us exactly how to "throw off" the temptation of this sin. He says, "Flee from sexual immorality"! Picture Paul yelling "Run away!" What other sin has destroyed so many families, churches, businesses? *Flee* this sin.

What other temptations might you have? Gossip? Maybe you need to choose better friends. Entertainment choices? You might need to cancel the cable.

Show them where you're heading

After throwing off the sin, we're told to run with perseverance, our eyes fixed on Jesus. We need to endure. And let your kids see you following Jesus as the perfect and final example.

That's one of the wonderful things about the Christian life—we have purpose. The author of Hebrews doesn't just tell us to "not do" various things. He provides a goal. We need to fix our eyes on Jesus. We need to get to know him better. How much time do you spend talking with Jesus each day? Reading the Bible? How did Jesus respond to others? How did he treat the poor? Children? Did he devote time to prayer?

As we get to know Jesus better, our lives will reflect it. Then our kids will witness this metamorphosis. They'll see your eyes are fixed on the only one who has ever lived a perfect life: Jesus.

WHY KIDS LIE

A few years ago *New York* magazine featured an article about why kids lie. In a study, Dr. Nancy Darling and her research team discovered that 98 percent of the teenagers studied reported lying to their parents. The most interesting aspect of this study was where the students learned to lie: *They learned it from their parents.*

Dr. Victoria Talwar, an assistant professor at Montreal's McGill University and a leading expert on children's lying behavior, explained this to the magazine: "We don't explicitly tell them to lie, but they see us do it. They see us tell the telemarketer, 'I'm just a guest here.' They see us boast and lie to smooth social relationships."[30]

I have a good friend who admittedly was a compulsive liar. When he first noticed the problem, he began to take note of how many times he lied daily. He easily counted five or six times per day, simple little lies, mostly exaggeration and editing of small details to be more convincing. Things like:

- "I spent an hour this morning cleaning up that mess." (In truth, it was only 20 minutes.)
- "Traffic was crazy. I've never seen it like that." (He left 15 minutes later than he should have. In reality, he only hit two stoplights. Traffic wasn't bad at all.)
- "I called her four times. Never got an answer." (He called once.)

When I talked with my friend, I asked him a little about his past. Eventually he began to share about his mom. "She lied all the time. We got used to it. It was a way of life for us."

He began to share story after story of his mother's "lies of convenience." She would lie to her friends about her son's performance at school and in sports. She would lie to her husband about the money she'd spent that day. She'd even involve the kids, telling them to lie about their ages when buying movie tickets to get the better price. Soon the kids learned this principle: *Lying gets you out of trouble! Lying gets you stuff!*

His mother's actions shaped his values. It was only in the last decade that he started putting God first in his life and allowing him to change the way he thinks.

LEAVING A LEGACY

Our actions shape our kids. We need to inspire by example. Whenever I'm goofing around in front of the kids, it seems that I always end up doing something that makes Lori sigh and say, "What kind of example are you leaving the kids with?"

It's an interesting question.

Have you thought about the example you leave? What about when your kids are gone and out of the house? What will they remember?

A few years ago my grandpa died. His funeral was a gathering of friends and family who came to celebrate a life well lived. I was one of the many who got a chance to share about the legacy my grandpa left. As each person shared, I was inspired by his example. People shared of his servant attitude, his compassion, and his heart for God. The man left a legacy of love and service.

Whenever I hear people give a eulogy about a loved one at a funeral, I can't help but think, *What would my family say about me?* I hope my kids would say, "He was always fun, he made me laugh, and he was always there for me." I fear that they could say, "He was intolerant of my mistakes!"

It's heartbreaking to think about leaving a legacy of anything less than unconditional love for my kids. I hope that my kids would see an example of God's love through me.

I hope that my wife would say, "Jonathan always made me feel loved."

I hope that my friends would say, "It was always easy to have good, clean fun around Jonathan. And at the same time, Jonathan was someone who inspired me to grow in my relationship with Christ."

Have you ever considered what kind of legacy you're leaving? Have you ever wondered what your kids would say about you when you're gone? What your family would say?

If only we could hear our eulogy now. Wouldn't that be sobering!

I'd like you to press pause for a second and go get a blank piece of paper. I'll wait.

Got it? OK, write "My Legacy" across the top of the paper. Now draw two vertical lines, creating three even columns on the page. At the top of the left column, write, "The Legacy I Desire to Leave for My Family." Leave the middle column blank for now. At the top of the right column, write, "The Legacy I Am Actually Leaving My Family!"

If you can be honest with yourself, this exercise can be eye-opening. Basically, you're writing your own eulogies—actual and possible—that your kids would give at your funeral. Think of it as a Dickens moment—you are now a character in *The Christmas Carol*. You are being given a chance to look at your present and your future, and the disparity that exists between the two.

Be specific as you fill out the chart. Don't just say, "He was a good dad!" or "She was a nice mom!" Provide details. "He always devoted time to his kids, despite his busy schedule." Or "She was the one I could go to whenever I had a problem if I wanted someone to listen."

Take a moment right now and fill out the left and right columns of that chart. Write in third person, as if others were saying these things about you.

Here's an example of how this can be done.

My Legacy

The Legacy I Desire to Leave for My Family

1 Dad always devoted time to us, despite his busy schedule.

2 Dad was patient when we messed up.

3 Dad was fun!

4 Dad taught me how to think biblically about my decisions.

5 Dad was a good husband to Mom, always letting her know how beautiful and special she was to him.

6 People liked having Dad around! He was warm and engaging.

7 Dad inspired people to live like Christ!

The Legacy I Am Actually Leaving My Family!

1 Dad was pretty good at devoting time to us, despite his busy schedule.

2 Dad was only patient with our mess-ups about half of the time.

3 Dad was fun!

4 Dad taught me how to think biblically about my decisions, but didn't always live it out.

5 Dad was a good husband to Mom, always letting her know how beautiful and special she was to him.

6 Most people liked having Dad around—as long as you didn't work in customer service for an airline!

7 Dad inspired people to live like Christ with his words! He didn't always with his actions.

If you haven't already filled yours out, go ahead and do it now. This is a great exercise because it forces us to do several things:

- It pushes us to think about what kind of legacy we desire to leave as a parent, a spouse, and a friend.
- It makes us think about our kids' perceptions of us. And that's important because, as most people know, *perception* is sometimes different from *reality*.
- It forces us to take an authentic look at the reality of our actions in each of these areas.

Now let's look specifically at the disparity between the legacy you desire and the actual legacy you are leaving.

If you look at my example, you'll notice that some weren't different at all. For example, my third entry—"Dad was fun!"—was the same in both columns. That means that I actually am meeting my goal of "being fun." For my family, that means being spontaneous, cheering them up when they're stressed or down, and trying my best to bring a heartfelt smile out of them throughout the day. In my perception, I think I actually succeed at that. My kids would probably agree.

But the gap between desired outcome and reality was immense at times, like my second entry. As much as I want to be patient all the time, in reality, I'm probably only patient with their shortcomings about 50 percent of the time. I don't usually overreact to their big mess-ups, but when they tell me they flossed their teeth . . . and they didn't, I might overreact.

This kind of impatience is a real problem. It probably builds a wedge between my relationships with each of my kids. If I continue to be impatient with them when they stumble, they will be more inclined to hide their failures from me when they mess up. After all, *they don't want to get Dad mad.*

That is an area where I can use some serious improvement. And, here's where the center column comes in. The purpose of this column is to help us identify how to get from actual reality to desired outcome. I want to be patient with my kids, but currently, I allow them to get under my skin. So how do I move from impatience to patience?

Let's look at another of my other shortcomings brought to light in this chart. In my first entry, I want my kids to feel that I always devoted time to them, despite my busy schedule. In reality, I had to write that I was only "pretty good" at doing this. I think I make a pretty noble effort to spend time with them. Currently, I take each of my girls to the cheap breakfast diner once a week, and Alec and I do weekly lunch (he's out early this semester of his senior year). Lori and I also do lots of family dinners, and we go to most of their sporting events. Lori and I probably would think we devote plenty of time.

BUT REMEMBER, THIS IS ALL ABOUT *THEIR* PERCEPTIONS, NOT OURS.

Often, Ashley asks me to go somewhere with her and I give her the proverbial "Not now, baby, I'm working." Alec asks me to play an Xbox game with him, and I give the same response. Their perception might be that I'm too busy at times. If our kids give the eulogy at our funeral and say, "Dad wasn't there for us!" we can't sit up in the coffin and yell, "I object! I spent plenty of time with you!" (Plus, that would be kinda freaky!)

So this is another area in which I can use some improvement. How do I move from being pretty good at spending time with them to a place where I really consider their needs above mine?

Here's where a whole Sunday school class of children would shout out that the answer is: "Jesus!"

I don't want to sound like I'm oversimplifying, but let's think about it. What *is* the better way to fix it? By our own efforts, or by submitting to God and letting him work through us?

In Philippians 2:3-5, Paul lays down a criteria for leadership that goes against all common sense. Here's what he writes: "Do nothing out of selfish ambition or vain conceit, but in humility consider others better than yourselves. Each of you should look not only to your own interests, but also to the interests of others. Your attitude should be the same as that of Christ Jesus."

The world often says, "If you want to make it to the top, you're going to have to step on a few people to get there!" But both Jesus and the apostle Paul introduced a totally different kind of leadership here. It's the kind of leadership where the last shall be first (Luke 13:30) and where the person of highest position in the room . . . *washes feet* (John 13:1-17)!

We are supposed to consider others better than ourselves, and rather than looking out for our own needs, we should look out for others first. What would this look like if dads and moms everywhere practiced this? I'll tell you what it would look like on my chart. Impatience would transform into patience. Selfishness would turn into generosity.

Let's document how we can do this in the center column of our "My Legacy" chart. Label the top of the center column, "Humble Efforts." I say "humble" because they aren't really from us, they're from God *in us*.

I want to look at what I could do to move from current reality to my desired outcome. On the chart, I'm going to list some "humble efforts" that will help me bridge that gap. I'll add those efforts to the center column now (see page 151).

If we walked away from this exercise unchanged, it would be a real shame.

As I look at my shortcomings, highlighted in the disparity between reality and my desired outcome, I see a glaring need to rely on God more and let his Spirit fill me with a joy that overflows to my family, friends . . . and even the airlines!

My Legacy

The Legacy I Desire to Leave for My Family!

1 Dad always devoted time to us, despite his busy schedule.

2 Dad was patient when we messed up.

3 Dad was fun!

4 Dad taught me how to think biblically about my decisions.

5 Dad was a good husband to Mom, always letting her know how beautiful and special she was to him.

6 People liked having Dad around! He was warm and engaging.

7 Dad inspired people to live like Christ!

Humble Efforts

1 I need to be proactive about doing activities my kids want to do with me, not just what I want. For Alec, that means playing video games; for Alyssa, board games; for Ashley, going on dates.

2 I need to spend more time in prayer asking the Holy Spirit to fill me with joy!

3 Keep seeking to serve their needs, not mine.

4 Praying consistently and seeking accountability to be authentic.

5 Keep seeking Lori's needs, not my own.

6 Spend time in prayer—especially before dialing the airline!

7 Again, prayer and accountability to be authentic.

The Legacy I Am Actually Leaving My Family

1 Dad was pretty good at devoting time to us, despite his busy schedule.

2 Dad was only patient with our mess-ups about half of the time.

3 Dad was fun!

4 Dad taught me how to think biblically about my decisions, but didn't always live it out.

5 Dad was a good husband to Mom, always letting her know how beautiful and special she was to him.

6 Most people liked having Dad around—as long as you didn't work in customer service for an airline!

7 Dad inspired people to live like Christ with his words! He didn't always with his actions.

What example are you leaving for your kids? What example would you like to leave? What humble efforts will get you from one place to the place where you really want to be?

Don't wait for your own funeral. Consider the difference you can make in the next week, the next month, the next year, and the next decade. There is no better time than the present.

• CANDID QUESTIONS FOR REFLECTION •

Some Questions for You, You & Your Spouse, or Your Small Group to Ponder

1. **SHARE A** time when you set a good example for your kids. (If you're going through this book solo, write your thoughts here.)

2. **SHARE A** time when you didn't exactly set a good example for your kids. (If you're going through this book solo, write your thoughts here.)

3. **FROM EARLIER** in this chapter: "Our Christian bumper stickers and T-shirts don't define us, our actions do." What attitudes and positive actions does the world—your neighbors, people at work, etc.—see when they watch you?

4. **WHAT NEGATIVE** actions do they see? How could following the challenge of Philippians 2:3-5 help?

5. **WHAT VALUES** do you want to live out and pass down to your kids? How's that going for you?

6. **WHAT ACTIONS** would you like to eliminate from your life so you don't pass them down to your kids?

7. **WHAT SHORTCOMINGS—SMALL** or glaring—did you observe in your "Legacy" self-evaluation?

8. **WHAT HUMBLE** efforts can you begin to work on this week? Specifically, what will that look like?

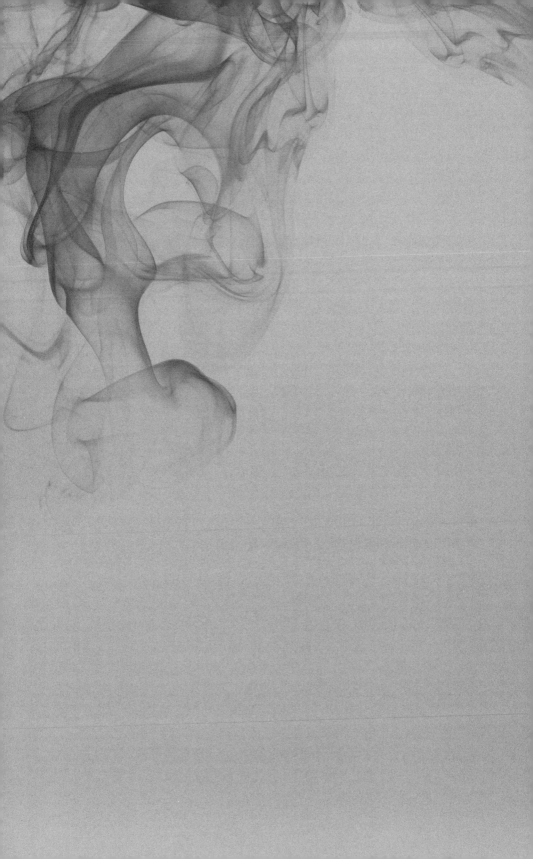

LETTING GO

BEFORE THEY'RE GONE

(RAISING UP DANIELS)

A TEENAGER STROLLED INTO A music store, pants sagging, his stylish mom trailing a few yards behind, chattering on her cell phone. He thumbed through a few CDs, paused, and his eyes fell on a particular title. He glanced over at his mom, who was licking her thumb and wiping lint off her $90 designer jeans, still engrossed in her cellular conversation. He turned his attention back to the CD, eyeballing the explicit lyrics label and contemplating his next move. After a deep breath, he quickly picked up the CD and marched confidently to the counter.

The attendant started to ring up the CD but hesitated, noticing the explicit lyrics label. He looked up at the teenager's mother, noticing that she was on the phone—and paused.

The boy looked up at his mom.

The young couple in line behind the boy began staring at the mom.

Mom finally noticed the hush, feeling the stare of four pairs of eyes. Awkwardly, she stopped her conversation and looked at the attendant. Holding the phone aside, she lifted her eyebrows as if to say, "Need something?"

The attendant robotically pronounced, "Ma'am, I'm supposed to inform you that this CD has explicit lyrics on it."

Silence.

The attendant waited, tapping his forefinger on the CD.

The teenager waited.

The young couple waited.

One could almost hear the clock ticking as the entire store waited in suspense.

The mom blushed and paused awkwardly for about five seconds, although anyone present would have sworn it was closer to an hour. Finally she blurted out, "Well, he's going to hear it at school anyway!" . . . and resumed her conversation.

Three minutes later, the boy exited the store with a smirk on his face, swinging a small plastic bag carrying his CD choice, his mother just a few steps behind, reimmersed in her conversation.

An hour later another teenager from the outskirts of the same city strolled into the same music store with his conservatively dressed mom just two steps behind him. This boy didn't even browse through any CDs; he just meandered up to the counter, expressionless.

The attendant asked, "What can I help you with?"

The boy looked up to his mom and waited. As if on cue, the mom smiled at the attendant and answered, "We're here to get Chris a CD," patting Chris on the shoulder proudly.

The attendant looked down at the boy and asked him, "What kind of music do you like?"

The boy sighed, stole a quick glance at his mom, and then reluctantly said, "Whatever she wants me to have."

Five minutes later, the kid exited the store, deadpan look, dangling a small plastic bag from two fingers—a bag carrying *The Best of John Tesh.*

TWO KIDS, SAME DAY, SAME STORE.
WHICH TEENAGER WOULD YOU RATHER HAVE? A REBEL, OR A ROBOT?

Do you have to settle for either?

SOLUTION: A SLOW SEGUE

In chapter 6, I referred to two parenting extremes: Shirley Shoebox and Sally SoWhat. One extreme shelters our kids from ever learning discernment. The other extreme doesn't provide any guidelines at all, exposing her kids to numerous harmful, yet easily avoidable influences.

Achieving a balance between these two extremes is always a struggle for parents. How much guidance is too much guidance? How much freedom is too much freedom?

The answer I would suggest: "a segue."

If you ask a radio DJ what a segue is, she'll probably tell you, "A dissolve from one song to another." One song fades out while the other fades in.

As kids grow up, parents need to learn to segue from "high guidance" to "low guidance." You want to be neither at the Shirley Shoebox extreme nor the Sally SoWhat extreme.

Whether our kids are age twelve or age seventeen, we need to think about this segueing process. After all, we aren't always going to be standing over their shoulders. It's sobering if you think about it. At eighteen, our teenagers can look us in the eye and say, "Hasta la vista, Mom and Dad!"

We have just eighteen years to build relationships with our kids, doing our best to teach and model lasting values. How are you equipping them for that day when they take off into the great big world on their own?

For much of this book I've been talking about guidelines and boundaries. To some, my guidelines may seem rather strict. Please allow me to speak to the other extreme. Some of us might need to start easing up on the controls. As our kids grow older, we need to let them start making some of their decisions *while* we are at their side. This might mean even letting them fail.

Did you ever teach your kid to ride a bike? Can you imagine how ridiculous it would be if our teenagers still needed us to run alongside them and balance them?

Dad, I'm going to Taylor's house. Can you please run alongside me while I go over there on my bike?

If you taught your kid to ride a bike, you eventually let go. You might even have watched him crash a time or two. As our teenagers grow up, we need to free them up to start making decisions on their own.

Last summer we went camping with a bunch of families from our church. Alec wanted to sleep in his own tent with some friends. We've let him sleep in his own tent before—right next to us! But this time he wanted to actually put up his tent at a spot about two hundred yards from our campsite.

At first, I almost instinctively said, "Nope! We're camping as a family. You sleep with us!" But then I thought about it. *Parenting is a slow segue.* He used to sleep in a sleeping bag right next to us. A year or two later, he was in the other half of the tent, on the kids' side (we have one of those big tents with the zipper wall in the middle). A year or two after that, he was in his own tent with our dog, his tent nudged right next to ours. The year after that, his own tent was about twenty feet from our tent.

The natural segue was to let him sleep with his friends two hundred yards away. After all, he had just turned seventeen. One year from that point, he could go pitch a tent in Europe if he wanted to, and there's nothing I could do about it!

Parents need to start this process when their kids are young. With tents, it's easy. It gets more difficult when the decisions involve girlfriends, boyfriends, cars, movies, and school dances.

Please don't misunderstand me when I say "free them up." I'm in no way hinting that you should free them from moral obligation. The freedom we are giving them is the freedom to make the right choices for themselves. Our rules might become lighter, but the biblical values we built the rules on shouldn't change. Values like . . . modesty.

When our girls were young, we bought all of their clothes. They didn't even have to be with us—we made all the decisions. Believe it or not, it was difficult at times to find modest clothes for little girls. Most clothing lines are pretty "hoochiefied," as I would call them, or "sexualized," to borrow the American Psychological Association's term.[31] But with enough effort, we usually found some pretty modest and cute outfits.

As the girls got into middle school, the pressure to fit in increased. We began dialoguing more about modesty. I explained to our daughters how their wardrobe choices affected guys.

This wasn't just a one-time conversation; it was ongoing. At times we would be watching TV or a movie and we'd see a guy on the screen reacting to a girl who was dressed in a risqué fashion.

I'D PAUSE THE MOVIE AND ASK THEM, "WHY IS THAT GUY FREAKING OUT?" I GAVE THEM THE OPPORTUNITY TO ANSWER.

Of course, Ashley's way of verbalizing it was, "Because she's dressed like a tramp!"

So I asked, "What defines dressing *trampy*? Short shorts? A spaghetti strap top?"

IN OTHER WORDS, THIS CONVERSATION IS AN ONGOING ONE.

Fortunately, other parents in our church were having these discussions as well. One particular family had developed some great guidelines for their girls: the *bend over* test and the *reach up* test. If one of the girls was wearing something questionable, the mom would say, "Bend over, then stand up, and reach to the sky." If she saw a bra or too much skin with either of those moves, the girls couldn't wear the outfit.

A number of the families in our church ended up adopting the *bend over* and *reach up* tests—and girls starting dressing in layers of camis and tanks!

During their middle school years, we would go shopping with the girls. We picked the clothes together, guiding them as they selected their outfits. They told us what was cute, and we helped them decide what was modest.

Now, we still shop with them, but we give them a lot more freedom. Just the other day Alyssa was wearing some jeans that I thought were too tight. I told her, "Alyssa, you're gorgeous, and your jeans are clinging to you so much that there are a dozen guys scratching on our front door right now."

She gave me the typical "Dad, stop it!"

But then I asked her, seriously, "Alyssa, baby. At what point do jeans become too tight?"

WE TALKED FOR A FEW MINUTES. THE CONVERSATION
ENDED WITH ME TELLING HER, "IT'S UP TO YOU."

Our guidance with our girls' wardrobe has been a segue from *we buy everything* to slowly releasing them to *make modest decisions on their own*. They aren't totally there yet. We still need to step in at times and say, "Sorry, Ashley, no!" "Sorry, Alyssa, you just flunked the *bend over* test."

We're still teaching the same values, but now we're letting our girls have more control making choices based on those values. After all, they'll be making these choices by themselves in just a few years. (Sniffle, sniffle.)

ON THEIR OWN

I was teaching a parenting workshop last fall and a woman came up to me afterward, crying. Wiping her eyes, she told me, "My seventeen-year-old son can't wait to leave!" I tried to comfort her, but she went on. "He actually texted me while I was here at this workshop. He texted: 'Only 10 more months.' He's letting me know that he's tired of the rules!"

Not all of us have kids who are counting down the days. But it's a fact. Someday they'll be on their own. How equipped will they be to make good decisions when we aren't standing over their shoulders?

How equipped would they be if they were plucked from you today?

The Bible tells the story of four teenage boys who were plucked from the safety of their godly upbringing and thrown into the middle of a pagan culture, left to decide their future for themselves. I'm speaking of Daniel and his three friends, Hananiah, Mishael, and Azariah.

It was six hundred years before Christ and, just as the prophet Jeremiah predicted (Jeremiah 32:26-32), Nebuchadnezzar, king of Babylon, overtook the city of Jerusalem and the surrounding area, known as Judah. He completely destroyed the temple, taking many of the sacred articles back to his own temples where the Babylonians worshipped numerous gods. In addition, he plucked Israel's finest young men, "young men without any physical defect, handsome, showing aptitude for every kind of learning, well informed, quick to understand, and qualified to serve in the king's palace" (Daniel 1:4). King Nebuchadnezzar ordered his chief court official to teach them "the language and literature" (also 1:4) of the Babylonians.

This experience must have been very distressing, even painful for these young teenagers. Not only did they see their city destroyed and their sacred temple ransacked, they were yanked from their friends and family and forced to serve the very king that had just wiped out their homeland.

If this weren't bad enough, this chief official also gave them new names. For a Jew, this was an incredible insult. Names carried meaning and reflected lineage. These teenagers might have wondered if there would be any future at all for the Israelites. Their land was now occupied by the enemy, their temple besieged, and their very history snatched away from them. To add insult to injury, the new names they were given reflected the made-up gods of Babylon.

So here they were—teenagers—taken away from the safety of their upbringing and thrust into a world of polytheism (belief in numerous gods) and pagan thought.

In their unique situation, there *was no* segue. It was just: *Monday—Israel; Tuesday—Babylon. Good luck!*

How would your teenagers do if that happened to them tomorrow? Would they "resolve" to not defile themselves?

I use that phrase because that's exactly what Daniel did, again and again. Near the beginning of the book he did it with something that didn't even seem like that big of a deal. "Daniel resolved not to defile himself with the royal food and wine, and he asked the chief official for permission not to defile himself this way" (1:8).

I can't help but be impressed by this teenager. We don't know all the specifics of why Daniel made this decision. Some say it was because the food was offered to the Babylonian gods. But that may not be a good argument, because the vegetables that he asked for in the following verses may also have been offered to the gods. Here's what we do know for certain: Daniel had been through a lot. He had been ripped from his home, his people . . . even his name. Daniel chose to hang onto something to set himself apart. Maybe even to remind himself that God was in charge of his future—no one else was.

That's powerful. He was just a teenager and he took a stand to not defile himself.

Later in the narrative, Daniel and his friends' stand for God led to some serious consequences, like a lions' den and a blazing furnace. They stood up for God, and God protected them.

An interesting aspect about the story of Daniel is that he didn't object to learning the language and literature of the Babylonians. A sheltered Jewish kid who obviously wasn't scared to take a stand for God didn't see harm in learning a little about the culture he was forced to live in.

Perhaps, having incredible knowledge of the Hebrew Scriptures, he remembered two other Jewish heroes who were put in similar situations: Joseph, whom God raised through the ranks, learning the Egyptian language and culture along the way; and Moses, learning the culture of the Egyptians in Pharaoh's palace.

Daniel lived in and studied a secular culture, but at the same time resolved not to defile himself.

It's amazing how much relevance this still has, two and a half millennia later. As parents, we consistently wrestle with how comfortable we should get with this culture. Some decisions might seem easy. C.S. Lewis books—*good*. Pornographic magazines—*not good*. That's an easy "resolve" for us. But what about literature that doesn't seem so clear-cut to some? J.K. Rowling books? The Twilight series? Stephen King books? Where do we draw the line?

Life is full of decisions like these that aren't so black and white. Should we allow our kids to go to public schools? Should we let them watch TV and movies? How comfortable should we get with our culture?

THE SOURCE OF HEALTHY DECISION MAKING

It's our job to equip our kids to be able to live in this world without conforming to this world (Romans 12:1, 2). To do this, it's probably not a good idea to react like either Shirley Shoebox or Sally SoWhat. Instead, we should look for ways to teach our kids and teenagers to rely on God to help them make healthy decisions in a very sick world.

That's the secret. Teaching them to rely on God.

If you miss everything else in this chapter . . . in this entire book . . . don't miss this. God wants us to rely on him and give him control. As our kids are growing and starting to make decisions on their own, we need to teach them to give God control. As we begin to give up control of our kids, we can release them to God.

The alternative to this is just a bunch of rules. We don't want to just teach our kids and our teens a bunch of rules and guidelines. Most teenagers don't like them anyway. Today's teenagers want to know *why* for everything.

Recently, I told Alyssa that I needed her to get her chores done on a Saturday. I didn't provide any reasoning. So the inevitable question came up.

"Why?"

I wanted to say, "Because I said so!"

But instead, I explained that I wanted her to be able to relax on Sundays. Besides, often she has the opportunity to hang out with family or church friends after church, and she probably didn't want to have to miss out on those experiences. She eventually agreed—but she, like our other kids, wanted to know the "why."

God doesn't want us to just blindly follow a bunch of rules. A group of people tried to live their lives that way in New Testament times. They were called the Pharisees and teachers of the law. They didn't care about "why"—they just followed the rules. Jesus basically called them a bunch of fakers, trying to look good on the outside while empty on the inside ("whitewashed tombs," in his words, from Matthew 23:27).

God doesn't want our kids to grow up to be good fakers like the Pharisees. Instead, he offers us something authentic, a relationship with him where he guides and helps us to make our decisions.

Galatians 2:20 speaks about this decision making process: "I have been crucified with Christ and I no longer live, but Christ lives in me. The life I live in the body, I live by faith in the Son of God, who loved me and gave himself for me."

GIVING GOD CONTROL

Galatians is a great book to study with our teenagers. I love seeing teenagers finally "get it" when they begin to understand that the "fruit of the Spirit" does not consist of "rules" that we're to try to follow. The fruit of the Spirit (Galatians 5:22, 23) is what flows out of us when we give God control and he lives in us.

Parents don't need to isolate their kids from the reality of this fallen world. They need to equip them to be Daniels, relying on

God to help them make healthy decisions in a very unhealthy world. When our kids turn eighteen, they very well could be thrown right into the middle of it.

Daniel and his buddies were probably much younger than that when they were plucked from the safety of their upbringing and thrust into Babylonian culture.

THEY SEEMED TO FIND A HEALTHY BALANCE. THEY DIDN'T DEFILE THEMSELVES AND SELL OUT TO BABYLONIAN WORSHIP IN ANY WAY, YET THEY DIDN'T OBJECT TO LEARNING BABYLONIAN LANGUAGE AND LITERATURE.

As our kids and teenagers grow up in this culture, we can help them find that balance, always anchored to God's truth, but at the same time not isolated from the people of this world that God might want us to reach out to.

What does this balance look like? Here's an example from my home.

Parents often ask my opinion regarding whether they should send their kids to a public school, a private school, or homeschool their children.

My Bible doesn't have a verse that says, "Thou shall homeschool" or "Thou shall sendeth them to private schools!" The Bible has some passages that tell us to be very careful who we surround ourselves with and other verses where God's people are encouraged to go and be a light in a dark world (Matthew 5:14-16). Jesus surrounded himself with an inner circle of believers, but consistently reached out to, and even hung out with, notorious sinners (Matthew 9:9-13).

My answer to parents regarding this schooling question is never a black-and-white one. I've met amazing men and women of God who went to public schools, some who attended private Christian schools, and some who were homeschooled. All three options can produce great people of faith, and all three can also yield the exact opposite.

We need to make sure our kids are surrounded with people of encouragement, people who will build them up in their faith

(Hebrews 10:24, 25; Ecclesiastes 4:9-12). But at the same time, we need to equip our kids and teenagers to follow Jesus' challenge to go and make disciples (Matthew 28:19, 20).

My way isn't the only way—by any means. Lori and I have tried our best to raise our kids by teaching them truth and surrounding them with good Christian influences but, at the same time, not totally removing them from secular society.

When Alec (my oldest) turned five, it wasn't long before we were faced with making the decision of where he would attend kindergarten. Having looked at private Christian schools, we visited the local public elementary school and were pleased with the teachers and the kids. A bit more background: when I was in junior high, my mom taught in a private Christian school. She went on to become a professor at California State University in Sacramento. We asked her wisdom on this matter about Alec, and in our particular situation, she steered us to public schools. (I've seen numerous cases where private school was a much better option. Situations vary). We enrolled Alec, and eventually enrolled his sisters at the same school.

WE MOVED A COUPLE OF TIMES, AND EACH TIME WE CHECKED OUT THE LOCAL SCHOOL, MET THE TEACHERS AND THE PRINCIPAL, PRAYED, AND MADE OUR CHOICE.

This sounds relatively simple.

Then Alec hit fifth grade.

That's when Alec starting getting bullied. Alec isn't an instigator or a troublemaker (like his dad). He's a relatively quiet and creative kid. But Alec's innocence also made him a prime target for some of the rougher kids in the school who weren't so innocent. We talked with his teachers and the administration. It didn't take long to realize that their "Our School Is Bully Free!" slogan was a load of . . . well, you fill in the blank, but I think you get my point.

We started praying hard. For the first time in six years, we were considering homeschooling Alec. At the same time, we had found a fundamental school that the district offered—a school with incredibly high test scores and an impeccable reputation, a school that required much more parental participation.

We visited that school and met with the principal. The kids at the school were much more innocent and creative—more like Alec. We would have switched him that second, but there was a waiting list.

Alec came home from the "bully free" school one day . . . crying. His entire class was making fun of him at recess. One girl looked him in the eyes and said, "You're so ugly—I don't know what your mother must think, having such an ugly kid!" (OK, I realize this is a dad talking, but the truth is, Alec was anything but "ugly." He was a cute kid . . . a great kid.)

I e-mailed all my friends and asked them to pray. That afternoon I told Lori, "I don't think we can keep him there. It's time to pull him out."

"And do what?" she asked, not knowing what I was thinking.

"I don't really know. Homeschool. Anything but this!"

I'm being completely candid when I tell you . . . it was at that point that . . . the phone rang. It was that amazing fundamental school. They had an opening.

God is good.

The next few years went really well for our kids. They all eventually got into that fundamental school. The teachers were great and a large number of the student body was made up of Christian kids from local churches. The school wasn't perfect, but no school is.

We didn't hit many more speed bumps until my middle child, Alyssa, entered seventh grade. Middle school was a rough place. I knew this firsthand, having been on campus, running campus ministries, and coaching on several campuses around the region. I had worked with middle school kids long enough to know what a pivotal age this is.

No matter where our kids went to school, they were exposed to negative influences. During this time we were proactive about getting them involved in church and finding a core group of friends who had a faith like theirs. They had school friends as well, but their inner circle of friends were believers.

A big part of parenting teens and tweens today is teaching them to surround themselves with good Christian friends, while at the same time equipping them to be a light to friends who don't know Jesus. I've seen people go to both extremes—with negative results. Some parents allow their kids to surround themselves with unbelievers. This almost always ends up in disaster. I've also met plenty of kids who don't have a single friend who is an unbeliever. These kids never learn how to be a light.

When Alyssa hit seventh grade, it was hard to provide her with good influences because she was so saturated with bad influences every day at school. One thing that was very disappointing for Lori and me was when the administration of our kids' middle school allowed some of these negative influences to flow freely. One way the school allowed this to happen was through the music they tolerated at lunch. The school played Top 40 hits on campus during the lunch hour, and—just as we talked about in chapter 6—the administration didn't really understand what "clean version" meant.

My kids came home frequently telling me, "Dad, guess what song they played today at school!" It was always both amusing and disturbing to hear our local public school's song choices over the years. One day, the school crossed the line with my daughter. In PE they began teaching the kids a new dance called the "Superman" dance. My jaw dropped when I heard Alyssa tell me that this was "required learning" for PE. The Superman dance was a dance that kids would perform to the song "Crank That" by a young rapper named Soulja Boy.

In the school's defense, they didn't have any clue what the lyrics meant. Now let me say here, I apologize in advance for how raw the following short description is. But I find it amazing how few people understand the meaning behind such lyrics. According to many lyric Web sites, the song's first line is, "Soulja Boy off in this ho." But even someone with no knowledge of slang probably would have recognized the words "bitch" and "ho" (slang for whore) throughout the song.

If they would have spent some time looking up some of the terms, they would have found far worse than "bitch" and "ho." The song keeps repeating the phrase "Superman dat ho."

There are slang Web sites that will define that term for you. To "Superman a girl" is to ejaculate on her back. This usually happens because a guy is mad at his girlfriend for not having sex with her. Then when a bedsheet sticks to her back, it sticks to her like a Superman cape.

Some try to defend Soulja Boy, arguing that he doesn't mean that when he repeats the phrase "Superman dat ho." But in the song he repeats the phrase "Super soak that ho" ten times and "Super soak that bitch" six times.[32] (Sorry to be the bearer of information like this, but somebody has to do it.)

In the song played at my daughter's school, every time he says the word "ho," the "clean version" says "Oh!"

I had seen the song on the charts before Alyssa's school ever played it. The song rode the #1 spot on Billboard and iTunes for months, and just when I thought the hype was over, they began teaching the dance as part of the curriculum in PE classes!

I called the administration. I had never done that before. I try to not be a whiner or complainer. But I was fed up. This was the last straw. Not only had my little girl been hearing songs every lunch hour about sex and hooking up, now she was being taught a dance song by a foulmouthed womanizer who was making millions off of uninformed parents who allowed their kids to download this kind of garbage.

Alyssa finished the few months she had left, and then we home-schooled her and her sister for the next year.

For Lori and me, this was the right move. We were given a year to build into our kids' lives 24/7. My dad, a retired pastor, was able to come over once a week and teach Bible. My mom took a morning off each week and taught English (not bad: my middle school girls were being taught English by a university professor). It was a great year. The next year, we enrolled Alyssa at the same high school my son Alec attended.

I share my whole story to make this point: Every parent is going to face different situations when making these kinds of decisions. We need to make sure that we base these decisions on solid biblical truths. Are we teaching our kids truth? Are we surrounding them with Christian influences? Are we equipping them for the real world?

LETTING GO

How many years do you have left with your kids? If you haven't started the segue yet, then there's no better time than the present!

Freeing them to make good decisions doesn't mean setting them up for failure. When they're sixteen, it's not time to move the TV with the premium channels into their bedroom. (Lori and I don't even get the premium channels anymore. We found them to be distracting. It's too easy to watch stuff that we shouldn't be watching.)

IF ADULTS NEED TO "FLEE" THIS STUFF (SEE 1 CORINTHIANS 6:18),
I PROMISE YOU THAT SIXTEEN-YEAR-OLDS DO!

Slowly release your kids, your teenagers, to start making good decisions on their own. Don't abandon values. Don't ignore wisdom. And don't remove accountability.

And when they're eighteen, it's really up to them, isn't it?

• CANDID QUESTIONS FOR REFLECTION •

Some Questions for You, You & Your Spouse, or Your Small Group to Ponder

1. **WHAT ARE** some examples in your parenting experience in which you have "segued" from "high guidance" to "low guidance"?

2. **NAME SOME** ways that you're already releasing your teenagers to start making decisions on their own.

3. **WHAT ARE** some of the values you'd like your kids to have learned and practiced before they leave the house?

4. **WHICH OF** these values are they reflecting already?

5. **WHICH VALUES** do you think they need to work on? Why?

6. **HOW CAN** you give your teenagers opportunities to succeed (or fail) at living out those values?

7. **IN WHAT** specific ways can you teach your teenagers to give God control?

8. **TEACHING YOUR** kids to surround themselves with good Christian friends, while at the same time equipping them to be a light to friends who don't know Jesus, is a balancing act. What specific things can help them maintain this balance in friends? How can you help them continue to walk in that balance?

AM I TOO LATE?

(LAST-MINUTE EFFORTS)

EVERY TIME I FINISH ONE of my parenting workshops, I make myself available to talk with parents and try to answer questions. After doing numerous workshops, I started to take note of repeat questions that seem to emerge again and again.

Of all the repeat questions, one floats to the top as the most common. It's probably asked by at least one parent per workshop, and that's why I felt the need to address it—the title of this chapter. The question is: *Am I too late?*

The question is usually worded something like this: "Jonathan, I love the principles of building relationships, discovering communicating arenas, and teaching values—all good advice. But my son is seventeen and I haven't done this yet. *Am I too late?*"

Sometimes the age of their kid is even older. A mom asked me, "My daughter is nineteen, but she moved back in with us. *Is it too late for her?*"

Other parents ask about their kids that are out on their own already. "My son is twenty and lives in an apartment with his friends. *Is it too late to build a relationship with him?*"

I won't keep you waiting.

The answer is always the same: "It's never too late!" You're never too late to build a relationship with your kid . . . even your twenty-two-year-old "kid."

Do you parent a sixteen-year old and a twenty-one-year-old differently? Do you use different methodologies for different ages when building relationships and teaching values? Absolutely. But there is one universal truth that is consistent regardless of our kids' ages. *Relationship first!*

RELATIONSHIP, RELATIONSHIP, RELATIONSHIP

Once I assure parents that they're not too late, they always ask me, "So what do I do now? After all, I haven't done any of this. Where do I start?"

The answer is always the same. "Start with the relationship."

We've already devoted a section of this book to building relationships (chapters 2-4). I'm not going to rehash it here. I just want to put the importance of building relationships in perspective, especially for parents who are wondering, *Am I too late to start this with my kids?*

I have several friends who lead parenting workshops, and we like to get together, share stories, and brainstorm tools that seem to help parents effectively. I'll never forget my friend Rick's story about Deborah (I've changed her name), a parent in his workshop.

Rick was teaching a four-week workshop at his church. On the first week he spent the entire time talking about building relationships. At the end of their time, he gave a homework assignment—go home, engage in conversation with one of your kids, and try to discover something about them that you never knew before. He clarified. "Don't just start asking them questions like a parole officer. Try to enter their world, dialogue with them, and discover something new."

All the parents were dismissed. Some of them seemed really excited about the assignment. But Deborah looked hesitant, worried even.

Rick was cornered by someone else with a question, so he never got a chance to talk with Deborah, who slipped out the back.

A week passed and parents returned to the parenting workshop, taking their seats. The time came to start. Rick noticed that Deborah wasn't there.

About one minute into the workshop, Deborah slipped into the back of the room.

Rick asked the group, "Who wants to share how your assignment went this week?"

A few hands immediately went up. A dad shared how he was able to find out a lot about his son's friends and favorite activities by just stopping for "FroYo" (Frozen Yogurt) on the way home from baseball practice. "He was skeptical at first," the father shared. "But I kept asking questions, and before I knew it, he wouldn't shut up."

A few other parents related their stories as well. Rick kept peeking over at Deborah to see if she seemed at all inclined to share her story. Part of him wondered if she even did the assignment.

Finally, after a long pause, Rick took a stab in the dark. "Deborah, did you get a chance to try my homework assignment?"

At first, Deborah seemed surprised that he called on her, but she quickly answered, "Yeah . . . but my situation was a little different."

Rick encouraged her to share. "We'd love to hear about it."

All heads turned toward Deborah. After a slightly awkward pause, Deborah spoke up. "I'm a single mom and for the last two years I feel like I've lost my son."

Rick said that you could hear a pin drop in the room.

Deborah continued. "I don't think we've actually had a conversation in the past ten months. We talk business, I tell him to do his chores, he grunts back . . . that's it! He'll be eighteen in a couple months, and frankly, I don't know what our future entails.

"So when you gave this assignment, I was pretty skeptical. But I thought, 'Hey. What do I got to lose? It can't get any worse!' So I began looking for opportunities to talk with him."

The entire class listened as Deborah told her story. "Monday, nothing came up. We barely saw each other. Tuesday—nothing. Wednesday, he had his friends over and I started to give up on the whole idea, but then something happened. He and his friends came into the living room where I was sitting—my son wanted to use the good stereo. It has better bass, according to him. I looked up at him and smiled and he looked at me kinda funny. Then he actually asked my permission to use the stereo."

Deborah went on. "I told him, 'Sure.' And he waited for me to leave the room, but I didn't move. I just kept flipping through my magazine. So they resumed what they were doing and started playing this really foul rap music.

"He plays it all the time," Deborah clarified, almost as an aside.

"This went on for about ten minutes, with the volume up to the roof. I kept thinking I should leave, but his friends were laughing and joking, occasionally bringing me into the conversation. I kept smiling, making comments every once in a while, and we actually started talking a little bit—just real surfacy stuff like, 'Who's this guy rapping?' and 'Wow, he really likes that word!' One of his friends, Mike, was really friendly and kept talking with me.

"Finally, when a song ended, I asked Mike, 'What's your favorite song?' Mike seemed excited by the request and cued up a song by a guy named Jay Z. To me, it just sounded loud and foul like the rest of the stuff. But Mike liked it.

"When that song ended, I asked my son, 'Zach, what's your favorite song?'

"Zach seemed shocked that I asked. But Mike said, 'Play it for her.' And he did. Just more of the same to me." Deborah laughed, and the class joined her.

"Soon, they tired of the music," Deborah shared. "And they left the room. I didn't even see them for the rest of the night."

Rick interjected. "So you found out his favorite song?"

"Yes, but that's not the cool part." The class seemed to grow excited as Deborah shared her victory.

"The next day," Deborah continued, "I was walking our dog, Chacha—he's a poodle. And all of a sudden I hear this car behind me blaring this loud music. I didn't turn, because I didn't want to stare, but the car pulls up next to me, so close that I thought it was going to hit Chacha.

"It was my son. He was leaning over, rolling down his window. He said, 'Hey mom, you gotta hear this.'

"I leaned in his car and he started pumping some really loud music littered with some of the foulest lyrics I've ever heard. Zach is all excited and he says, 'Mom, this is the same guy I played you yesterday. I love this song.'"

Rick said that Deborah paused her story, lifting her hand to her lip, trying to stop herself from getting choked up, but it was too late. A tear rolled down her cheek.

She continued. "And then, with foul music filling our ears . . . he smiled at me."

She wiped her tears with the back of her sleeve.

"I can't remember the last time he smiled at me. It was the best moment we've had in years."

DESPERATE TO CONNECT

When Rick told me that story, in vivid detail, I couldn't keep myself from tearing up.

Rick and I agree, we're so proud of Deborah for making that effort to connect with her son.

AN ODD CONNECTION? DEFINITELY. BUT IN SHEER DESPERATION, DEBORAH ENTERED HER SON'S WORLD.

Maybe the brilliance of her connection was because she truly felt like she had nothing to lose. Zach was out of control, he was just months from having the freedom to leave and do whatever he desired, so with that glaring reality in the forefront of her mind, she reached out to try to make a connection. An onslaught of f-words later, she had a moment with her son.

Have you ever felt like Deborah? Have you ever been desperate to connect with your kids but you didn't know where to turn?

A dad approached me after a workshop, crying. He said, "I don't know what to do with my son. I just hope it's not too late!"

I was able to step aside with him so we could talk privately. I asked him, "What's going on?"

Lowering his voice, he shared that his son had been flirting with pornography and "sexting" girls (sending sexual text messages).

I asked, "How did you respond?"

"Alright, I guess," he answered. "I caught him looking at Internet pornography on my computer. He apologized to me, but then two days later, we caught him sending sexual texts to a girl he met at school."

He described some of the detail of what his son had told this girl, and how she had replied. The situation grew out of control. The girl's mother looked at her phone and saw their conversation. The mom texted this guy's son back, typing, "If you ever text my daughter again, I'm calling the police."

This father told me story upon story in which his son was making stupid decisions.

I finally asked him, "How would your son describe his relationship with you?"

He paused, contemplating my question. "Pretty good, I guess."

I probed, "Do you get any regular time with him, just to talk, father to son? A time where you can listen to him and hear his heart?"

He squirmed in his chair a little bit as I asked these detailed questions about his relationship. Speaking candidly, he said, "Not a regular time. We talk a little on the way to lacrosse practice, that's all."

So I gave him the advice that I give every parent. "Relationship first!"

Parents, especially parents who feel like they're "losing my kid" (I hear it all the time), need to focus on the relationship.

I can't help but think of 1 Corinthians 13, the love chapter.

> If I speak in the tongues of men and of angels, but have not love, I am only a resounding gong or a clanging cymbal. If I have the gift of prophecy and can fathom all mysteries and all knowledge, and if I have a faith that can move mountains, but have not love, I am nothing. If I give all I possess to the poor and surrender my body to the flames, but have not love, I gain nothing.
>
> Love is patient, love is kind. It does not envy, it does not boast, it is not proud. It is not rude, it is not self-seeking, it is not easily angered, it keeps no record of wrongs. Love does not delight in evil but rejoices with the truth. It always protects, always trusts, always hopes, always perseveres. Love never fails (1 Corinthians 13:1-8).

In this chapter, Paul said some pretty daring stuff. He basically said, "You can be a prophet, you can do miracles, you can be Mr. Super Faith guy . . . but if you don't love, then you are nothing but an irritating gong that people just want to silence!"

Wow! This is so relevant to us parents. We can have wonderful guidelines, we can teach devotions better than anyone in the church, we might even buy our kids the best toys that money can buy, but if we don't make them feel loved—*GONG!!*

All our rules and guidelines are pointless if we don't devote time just loving our kids for who they are.

CANDID CONFESSION # . . .

Last fall Alyssa and I had a pretty severe disagreement. I finally told her the way it was going to be and she stomped off and said, "Figures!"

Stab!

That hurt worse than anything I felt in a long time. One simple word. A word that probably meant, "This type of unfair punishment is typical of you, Dad!"

Ouch!

I could only sit still for about five minutes and then I decided that I'd go up to her room and talk with her.

When I got to her room, she was sitting on the floor doing homework. Rather than talking about the issue at hand, I asked her about homework, school, water polo, her friends at church, and a few other things. After sharing a few facts with me about her homework load and her friends, I said, "Wow, I didn't know that."

She quickly retorted, "I know!" in a snippy tone of voice, as if to say, *Yes, you don't understand me!*

My lack of understanding of my daughter was saying one thing to her: *GONG!!*

I thought about it for a moment. Alyssa and I used to go to breakfast together every other week. (I alternated with her and her sister.) Their schedules changed, and we stopped for a while, with the full intention of resuming the breakfasts again soon. But as I sat there in Alyssa's room pondering the situation, I realized that it had been over a year since we'd had our weekly breakfasts. And in actuality, her snippy little comment to me was pretty accurate. I *didn't* know her as well as when we were having those regular breakfasts.

Embarrassed, I asked her some questions, seeking clarification. "So, you feel like I don't understand you?"

She didn't hesitate for a nanosecond. "You don't!"

GONG!!

I continued. "You think I'm treating you unfair, based on this lack of knowledge?"

"Yes!" she said, a little nicer this time, but with a tone of, *Are you up to something?*

I had decided what I needed to do. So I proposed it to her, beginning with an apology. "Lyssy, I'm sorry."

She didn't respond. So I continued.

"I want to understand you and I want to be fair with you. So I've got an idea."

She looked up at me curiously.

"I want you to make a list," I suggested. "I want you to write, 'I wish my dad would . . .' and then finish the sentence. Write as many things as you want. Just list them out. Then let's meet for breakfast tomorrow and I'll hear you out."

ALYSSA WASN'T JUMPING FOR JOY WHEN I MADE THE BREAKFAST OFFER.

That's one of the more difficult aspects of being a parent of a teenager. When they're kids, you mention breakfast and it's like, "Oh boy! Breakfast!" Then they hit the teenage years, and a creature takes over their body. What used to be "Oh boy!" becomes, "So?"

Right now my two oldest have already entered that phase. Ashley hasn't hit it yet. She and I joke with each other about it. She says, "Daddy, I'll never turn into an emotional monster!"

Of course, she always says this right in front of Alyssa. But Alyssa is a teenager, so she just shrugs her shoulders and says, "Whatever."

I always whisper to Ashley, "Don't turn over to the dark side!"

Anyway, my sweet little creature Alyssa and I went to breakfast the next morning and had a blast. I didn't have any agenda other than *relationship first*. So we just talked. I asked her questions and she loved the opportunity to talk freely.

In my years of youth ministry, I've noticed that about teenagers. In groups, some teenagers are very quiet. When you get them one-on-one and engage them in conversation, they gab for hours without taking a breath!

I've had some adults tell me, "Jonathan, my kid won't talk!"

Sure, there are exceptions. But the majority of kids will talk if they find someone who is truly interested in listening.

Sadly, I've observed some of these adults who claim that kids won't talk. I've seen these adults simply lecture their kids. There's a huge difference between a *lecture* and a *two-way conversation*. Adults who err on the side of listening more than talking can eventually get a kid to start talking.

After Alyssa and I talked for a while, I asked her, "So, do you have a list for me?"

She smiled and proudly pulled the list out of her purse.

What happened the next twenty minutes was absolutely amazing.

Alyssa shared one of her concerns. Then I asked her questions about her concern, trying to draw her toward the answer. For example, one of her items on the list was, "I wish Dad wouldn't freak out whenever I want to hang with my friends from school."

I responded with a simple question. "Define 'freak out.'"

She tried to explain it and had trouble putting it to words. Here's where I had to be really careful. I'm pretty good at being condescending (it's my spiritual gift). So I treaded carefully, and instead of saying, "Well, seeing that you have no evidence of this offense . . . " I tried the old St. Francis of Assisi principle of seeking first to understand before being understood.

I offered, "So you feel like I jump on your case every time you want to be with your school friends that aren't believers?"

Her face lit up, and she yelped, "Exactly!"

It's kind of funny if you think about it. All I had to do was keep my mouth shut, not be condescending, and repeat back what she said to me. Psychology 101 at work.

Feeling a little bit understood, she explained her concern. "Dad, you don't want me to hang out with school friends because you're afraid that I'm going to start being like them. First, most of them aren't bad. Second, I'm not stupid. I'm not going to start becoming like them just because I hang out with them once."

I had to be careful once again. Part of me wanted to argue with every little "bullet point" that she maintained. I didn't agree with a lot of what she said. But by some miracle of God, I just asked, "So, what do you think I should do?"

She stopped for a second and thought. I think she was surprised that I was letting her come up with a possible solution—a great little parenting principle, by the way. If you have no idea what to say, ask them, "What do you think I should do about this?"

<hr />

COMEBACK QUESTIONS WORTH ASKING

Are you ever stumped by your teenager? They ask you something or tell you something and you have no idea how to respond?

Try some of these "comeback" questions that return the ball to their court. They accomplish two things: first, they give you time to think; second, they give teenagers a chance to use some problem-solving skills! It's a win-win!

1. What do you think you should do about that?
2. How do you think I should respond to that?
3. How's that working for you?
4. Define _____ (insert the word or phrase they just used).
5. So what does that look like?
6. So what do you suggest?
7. How will you be able to do that successfully?
8. How can I help you do it well?

<hr />

Alyssa decided against answering the question and instead opted to peel back another layer of herself. "Dad, I just wish you would trust me. I'm not out smoking pot and having sex. Neither are my school friends. It doesn't hurt to hang out with them a little bit. I spend way more time with my church friends. You should be glad."

I decided to put the ball in her court again. "So what do you think the balance looks like—time spent with school friends vs. church friends?"

Alyssa articulated, "I think that my closest friends should be my church friends. They are the ones that really understand me anyway. They understand my relationship with God. But I think it's OK to have school friends too. They're just not my closest friends."

I was so proud of my little girl. I decided to repeat back to her to make sure I understood, and to make sure *she knew* I did. "So you're saying, as long as your inner circle of friends are believers, then they can encourage you in your relationship with God, keeping you accountable. Then you can have some casual school friends as well. Kids that hopefully you will impact." I took the liberty of using slightly different semantics when summarizing her thoughts.

She responded eagerly. "Exactly."

So I put the ball in her court again. "You and I have both seen kids who allow people to influence them for the worse. And you have read passages of Scripture that tell us to surround ourselves with believers who will encourage you in your faith. How will you be able to keep yourself in check with these principles?"

Then my little girl impressed the socks off of me. She said, "I think I need to keep church a priority. I shouldn't let sports or hanging out with school friends ever interfere with Wednesday nights or Sundays (the two times her youth group meets). Also, I should find someone that I can talk to about this, like Heidi or Natalie, and make sure that they help me to not mess up."

I was completely surprised. To be honest, I don't think I could have come up with a better answer myself. Unintentionally, she had just preached a two-point sermon.

"Alyssa," I said, "That was an incredibly wise answer."

She smiled. "Thanks, Daddy."

"You basically are saying that you want to keep church a priority," I clarified. "And secondly, you want to connect with a believer who will keep you accountable to surrounding yourself with a good Christian influence."

"Yep," she said contently.

We spent the next few minutes talking about what that might look like, then we went through the next four items on her list. By the time we finished, she had pretty much resolved every issue for herself. I thanked her for sharing the list with me.

It was a great experience for both of us. Before that breakfast, she didn't know that I was willing to trust her on some of the issues she shared. I *was* willing to trust her—I just needed to dialogue with her about it and know her thoughts.

> ## ONCE WE TALKED, I WAS MORE IMPRESSED WITH HER THAN
> ## I EVEN REALIZED, AND SHE WAS SURPRISED WITH HOW MUCH FREEDOM I
> ## WAS WILLING TO GIVE HER IF WE COMMUNICATED. IT WAS A TWO-WAY STREET.

There's nothing magical about breakfast. But there is something amazing about communication. Alyssa's willingness to share, and my willingness to listen, brought us closer together in just one breakfast. We've been having these breakfasts weekly since. (I've resumed coffees with Ashley too. Alec and I already meet for lunch once a week.)

Something I don't want you to miss: I had to prove my willingness to listen before Alyssa opened up and talked. As parents, we need to demonstrate our desire to understand our teenagers before they will trust us enough to get vulnerable and share a part of themselves. If we don't show a willingness to understand them, then they'll close up. They don't want to offer information if it's only going to be used against them.

Relationship first!

NEVER TOO LATE FOR BOUNDARIES

If you are asking, "Is it too late?" are you also wondering if you should just forget about boundaries altogether?

Not at all.

It's "relationship first," not "relationship only."

A mom approached me after one of my parenting workshops and asked, "Do you think I should look at my son's Facebook account if he leaves it on?"

I was a little surprised by the question. So I clarified, "How old is your son?"

"He's sixteen."

"And you don't have his password?" I asked.

She looked surprised. "No. He won't give it to me."

I paused for a moment, contemplating how to respond. "Do you really want to know what I think?" I finally asked.

"Yeah," she said, matter-of-factly.

"Who is the parent here?" I asked her honestly.

Parents need to set boundaries. I think some parents are scared that if they set any rules or guidelines, it will ruin the relationship. It won't.

Yes, the relationship is the first priority. But that doesn't mean we should throw our values out the window. It's still OK to say, "This doesn't belong in my house."

Boundaries can be tough to enforce at times. The same Alyssa that was an angel at that breakfast was the brood of Satan two weeks later when she didn't clean her bathroom and I called her on it. It turned into a huge ordeal and no matter what I tried, she argued. I had to eventually walk away and just assure her, "I love you, baby, and you're going to do your chores and not argue about it. Someday you may look back on this and see the value of it."

Usually my kids come back later (if not days, years!) and say, "I see why you made me clean the stupid bathroom!"

In my house the big battles aren't over alcohol and sneaking out . . . they're over flossing your teeth and cleaning bathrooms. We're a weird family!

Relationships first, then boundaries.

And remember . . . it's never too late to start being a parent.

• CANDID QUESTIONS FOR REFLECTION •

Some Questions for You, You & Your Spouse, or Your Small Group to Ponder

1. **HOW WOULD** you complete the homework assignment, "Engage in conversation with one of your kids, and try to discover something about them that you never knew before"?

2. **WHY DO** you think Deborah's son Zach was willing to share his music with her?

3. **DESCRIBE A** time where you had a "moment" with one of your kids, a time where they connected with you.

4. **HOW CAN** you make the relationship with your kids first priority?

5. **WHAT ARE** some ways in which our love for our kids is drowned out by a resounding "GONG!!"?

6. **WHICH OF** the comeback questions have you used successfully in talking with your kids and teenagers? Are there other comeback questions you've used? What are they?

7. **WHAT ARE** some specific ways that you can prove you're willing to not only listen, but also to seek to understand?

8. **WHAT ARE** some ways that you can enforce boundaries without "clanging" or "gonging" and showing a lack of love?

9. **IF YOU** had a friend who told you it was *too late* to parent his teenager properly, how would you answer her or him?

A LETTER FROM JONATHAN

WHILE WE'RE ALL IN THE mode of being completely honest, let me share one more confession: my kids are one of the greatest joys in my life!

Have you ever read the verses that follow the well-known lines in that famous "build your house" passage in Psalm 127?

> SONS ARE A HERITAGE FROM THE LORD,
> CHILDREN A REWARD FROM HIM.
> LIKE ARROWS IN THE HANDS OF A WARRIOR
> ARE SONS BORN IN ONE'S YOUTH.
> BLESSED IS THE MAN
> WHOSE QUIVER IS FULL OF THEM (PSALM 127:3-5).

I can't agree more. My kids are complete blessings.

Don't get me wrong. I've wanted to kill each one of my kids at one time or another. (Especially when they first hit puberty! They were monsters!) And they probably wanted to kill Dad a few times too. But those times don't begin to faze the love I have for my kids, not in the least.

It's so amazing to see a little bit of me, and a little bit of Lori, woven into each of my kids. And all three are so diverse (at times, it's just weird!). Each are truly a reward from God.

If you've ever doubted that feeling of love toward your kids . . . maybe during a fight, or when your son wrecked your car while texting . . . all of those feelings of frustration and anger are swept away in an instant if their life is endangered. One call from a hospital reveals how trivial your kids' imperfections are. So remember that . . .

. . . Our kids are truly blessings.

JONATHAN

NOTES

1. Joel Rubinson, "Death of a Salesman, Starring Tiger Woods," *Fast Company*, http://www.fastcompany.com/blog/joel-rubinson/brave-new-marketing/death-salesman-starring-tiger-woods (accessed December 3, 2010).

2. http://www.quotedb.com/quotes/3069 (accessed December 3, 2010)

3. http://www.kff.org/entmedia/upload/8010.pdf (accessed December 7, 2010)

4. Ross Campbell, *How to Really Love Your Child* (Colorado Springs: Victor Books/ ChariotVictor Publishing, 1992 revised edition), p. 16.

5. "The Importance of Family Dinners VI," CASA, New York, NY, September 2010, http://casafamilyday.org/familyday/files/media/The%20Importance%20of%20Family%20Dinners%20VI%202010%20-%20FINAL.pdf (accessed December 6, 2010).

6. Ibid.

7. http://www.ucg.org/booklets/FM/influence.asp

8. Steve Farrar, *Finishing Strong: Finding the Power to Go the Distance* (Sisters, OR: Multnomah, 1995).

9. Ibid., 53.

10. Personal letter to the author; permission to publish granted by Brian Bixler to the author, November 21, 2010.

11. http://www.thesource4ym.com/archives/archivestore/2002/arc20020205.aspx#TITLE2 (accessed December 6, 2010)

12. "Youth Happiness Study," The Associated Press-MTV Study, http://surveys.ap.org/data/KnowledgeNetworks/2007-08-20%20AP-MTV%20Youth%20Happiness.pdf (accessed December 6, 2010).

13. Walt Mueller, *Engaging the Soul of Youth Culture: Bridging Teen Worldviews and Christian Truth* (Downers Grove, IL: InterVarsity Press, 2006), p. 26.

14. Study conducted by Annenberg Center, University of Southern California, http://www.csmonitor.com/Innovation/Horizons/2009/0616/is-the-internet-cutting-into-family-time (accessed December 7, 2010).

15. Victor C. Strasburger, MD, "Sexuality, Contraception, and the Media," http://www.pediatrics.org/cgi/content/full/126/3/576 (accessed December 7, 2010).

16. http://people.umass.edu/schalet/Contexts%202010.pdf (accessed December 7, 2010)

17. http://www.bimmerfest.com/forums/archive/index.php/t-50721.html (accessed December 7, 2010)

18. "Is Social Networking Changing Childhood?", Common Sense Media, August 2009, http://www.commonsensemedia.org/teen-social-media?utm_source=newsletter08.13.09&utm_medium=email&utm_campaign=feature1 (accessed December 7, 2010).

19. "Cause for Concern: National Study Shows Reversal in Decade-Long Declines in Teen Abuse of Drugs and Alcohol," study by the Partnership for a Drug-Free America and the MetLife Foundation, article on PR Newswire, http://www.prnewswire.com/news-releases/cause-for-concern-national-study-shows-reversal-in-decade-long-declines-in-teen-abuse-of-drugs-and-alcohol-85939067.html (accessed December 7, 2010).

20. Rich Campbell, "Parents Set the Bar Low, Enabling Kids to Belly Up," T.C. Palm News, January 14, 2009, http://www.tcpalm.com/news/2009/jan/14/rich-campbell-parents-set-bar-low-enabling-kids-be/ (accessed December 7, 2010).

21. "In the Ruins of El Toro," *Independence Day*, Blu-ray, directed by Roland Emmerich (2008, 20th Century Fox).

22. Steve Reinberg, "One in 4 Teen Girls Has a Sexually Transmitted Disease," *U.S. News and World Report*, posted March 11, 2008; http://health.usnews.com/usnews/health/healthday/080311/one-in-4-teen-girls-has-a-sexually-transmitted-disease.htm (accessed December 7, 2010).

23. Strasburger, "Sexuality, Contraception, and the Media."

24. American Academy of Pediatrics, 2009 report, http://pediatrics.aappublications.org/cgi/reprint/peds.2009-2146v2 (accessed December 7, 2010).

25. Kaiser Family Foundation report, http://www.kff.org/entmedia/upload/8010.pdf, p. 29.

26. American Academy of Pediatrics, 2009 report.

27. Kaiser Family Foundation report, p. 1.

28. Study for *Pediatrics* magazine, published August 2006, http://www.chron.com/CDA/archives/archive.mpl?id=2006_4165928 (accessed December 7, 2010).

29. http://www.casacolumbia.org/templates/PressReleases.aspx?articleid=451&zoneid=56 (accessed December 8, 2010)

30. Po Bronson, "Learning to Lie," *New York* magazine, February 10, 2008, http://nymag.com/news/features/43893/ (accessed December 9, 2010).

31. "Sexualization of Girls," American Psychological Association, http://www.apa.org/pi/women/programs/girls/report.aspx (accessed December 9, 2010).

32. http://www.anysonglyrics.com/lyrics/s/Soulja-Boy/Crank-Dat-Soulja-Boy.htm (accessed December 9, 2010)

ADDITIONAL PARENTING RESOURCES FROM STANDARD PUBLISHING

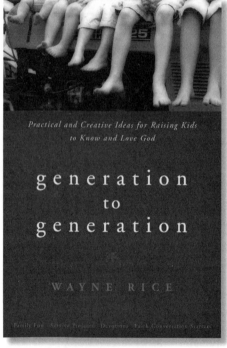

Generation to Generation
By Wayne Rice
Item # 021535410

Opie Doesn't Live Here Anymore
By Walt Mueller
Item # 24332

Visit your local Christian bookstore or www.standardpub.com

Standard®
P U B L I S H I N G